Coming to Life

Coming to Life

Traveling the Spiritual Path in Everyday Life

Polly Berrien Berends

1817

Harper & Row, Publishers, San Francisco

New York, Grand Rapids, Philadelphia, St. Louis
London, Singapore, Sydney, Tokyo, Toronto

FIRST EDITION

Library of Congress Cataloging-in-Publication Data
Berends, Polly Berrien.
    Coming to life : traveling the spiritual path in everyday life /
Polly Berrien Berends — 1st ed.
        p.   cm.
    Includes bibliographical references.
    ISBN 0–06–250062–7
    1. Spiritual life.   I. Title.
BL624.B46   1990   89-46148
248.4—dc20   CIP

---

90 91 92 93 94 HAD 10 9 8 7 6 5 4 3 2 1

This edition is printed on acid-free paper that meets the American National Standards Institute Z39.48 Standard.

To Price and Connie
and what they stand for:
that love is worth it.

Geese appear high over us,
pass, and the sky closes. Abandon,
as in love or sleep, holds
them to their way, clear
in the ancient faith: what we need
is here. And we pray, not
for new earth or heaven, but to be
quiet in heart, and in eye,
clear. What we need is here.

Wendell Berry

Contents

Preface   xi

Acknowledgments   xiii

1   Finding the Road That Leads to the Road   1

2   Dying to Wake Up   9

3   Is There Life Beyond Coping?   22

4   Yearning to Make Connections   36

5   Seeing Through Life's Betrayals   48

6   The Illusion of Growing Up   56

7   Discovering a Spiritual Viewpoint   67

8   Guided by Living Compasses   80

9   Universal Firsthand Realizations of Oneness   93

10   The Need to Be Reminded   110

11   False Prayer: Avoiding the Void   127

12   At Prayer and Aware: Dynamics of True Prayer   137

13   The Practice of Prayer   161

14   Now See Here   170

Notes   183

Preface

In you as you are and in your life just as it is happening right now is a wonderful spiritual dimension that needs only to be recognized. To engage in this spiritual awakening makes life at least tolerable, at most marvelous. We may begin by wishing things were different; we can progress to taking, even welcoming, life as it comes.

To look for the good in some other circumstance than the one in which we find ourselves is to trash the only happiness we will ever have: now. Whether it pleases us or not, each moment is a gift. No matter how unpleasant the wrapping, inside is something wonderful that life wants to give us. If we let it pass without opening it, we have missed something priceless. I hope this book will help some people to open more of their gifts.

It is not that suffering will end. As far as I can tell, the one thing we can count on is that everything we are counting on is going to fall through under us. I will never welcome the feeling of falling through the floor. But I believe we are falling through into God or something—but not nothing. I believe it is the whole from which we came and to which, deep down, we long to belong. I believe our longing is exceeded only by its longing for us. I have found some ways of going along with this process. This does not do away with pain, but it makes it possible to be less afraid, hurt, angry, and held back—more assured, free, and, finally, loving. I hope this book helps you find your way.

It is true that we exaggerate small hardships. But it is also true that we are afraid to admit to our real suffering. If we are not bleeding or starving, we think we are weak to feel as unhappy and alone as we sometimes do. But our aloneness and hurt are the same as the great loneliness that led to all great spiritual wisdom and literature. Our sufferings are our doors to spiritual awakening. I hope this book helps you to feel less flawed, and less alone, and to walk through some of your doors.

We would all like to trust more, and we can. We know more than we think we do. We can trust ourselves more than we do. We can trust life more than we do. There are laws of being that can be unearthed and counted on. When things go well, we are properly oriented. You can discover how when things don't go well you are disoriented. You can learn how, spiritually, to re-orient and come into better alignment with life. In this way I hope this book helps you discover that there is something be-yond self and other that you can trust.

Each of us is familiar with certain traditional spiritual ideas, which have much greater application to our lives than we realize or have been taught. These, too, are gifts that have to be opened, just as nuts have to be shelled. Whatever your tradition, I hope this book helps you to find firsthand how what you believe is so, and how it applies to every moment of your life.

Acknowledgments

My deepest gratitude goes to Leslie McKenzie, Barbara Greene, Price Berrien, Jody Blatz, Okke Postma, Jethro Lieberman, Gerard J. Koster, and Hugh Van Dusen for a host of important contributions—wise counsel, loving encouragement, and generous, thoughtful time taken to figure out what I was trying to say and to help me say it better. Writing can be a lonely business; you made it less lonely. Writing is an uncertain business; you made it clearer. This book was a long time in coming. Thank you for standing by me.

At Harper & Row I thank Roland Seboldt for shepherding this book into the fold; Ron Klug for insightful editorial suggestions; Robin Seaman for her wonderful enthusiasm and energetic commitment to spreading word of its existence; John Shopp for his clarity and support; Wendy Chiu for superb and caring assistance with corrections; and Hilary Vartanian, as well as others whose names I do not know, for many various contributions that brought *Coming to Life* to life as a book. It is wonderful to have teammates.

I thank my family for living through *Coming to Life* with me, from question to question, from confusion to love.

I thank all my students and clients, who make my learning more than personal, whose living contributions make this book more than an autobiography.

I am thankful for all who went before, the "scattered brotherhood" and sisterhood whose markings and remarkings comfort, inspire, and guide me daily.

Coming to Life

1. Finding the Road That Leads to the Road

One in all,
all in one.
If only this is realized,
No more worry about your not being perfect.

BUDDHIST SCRIPTURES

Pear seeds grow into pear trees, nut seeds into nut trees, and God seed into God.

MEISTER ECKHART

Instead of, "How much longer until we get there?" our children learned to ask, "How many roads?" Carefully counting on my fingers, I would reply, "We are on the road that leads to the road that leads to the road that leads to the road to Grandma's house." With this much to go on, they found patience possible. When at last we took the exit off the long turnpike, the joy of subtracting one road from the count was delicious. "Now," they shouted, "we are on the road that leads to the road that leads to the road to Grandma's house!"

Before you get on a train you have a right to know its destination. You may not know how the journey will be or what you will find when you get there, but you can have a general idea of the route to be traveled. Before you read this book, you have a right to know where it is going and, roughly, what you will have to go through to get there—what road leads to what road.

Tom stopped coming for counseling because he couldn't afford to pay. He left angry at me for letting him get so behind in his bills. Now, ten years later, he is back. His hair is slightly gray, but he is still the picture of a *puer aeternus*—an eternal boy. Why has he come? He tells of not being able to manage, of bouncing checks, of being late to work, of a promising, creative career that, due to fear-filled procrastination, remains unlaunched. He lives in other people's houses doing yard work in lieu of paying rent.

He has twice come close to marriage, but put off commitment, finding each prospective bride in some way inadequate. Both women have found others to love. Does he think he made a mistake? He nods and sucks in his breath. Sobbing, he speaks of loneliness, of missing his brothers and sisters and parents, of how sad it is that they don't have more time for each other.

What does he mean by love? What is it he misses? Weeping convulsively, he speaks of his yearning for someone to hold him at night, to tell about his day. In counseling he sees that his is a child's "carry me" idea of love. He finds being a grown-up too hard and yearns to return to childhood, yet he is now too big to crawl into anyone's lap. No relationship can meet all his demands, so each eventually betrays him, crumbling under the weight of his reliance. In fact, what he seeks in love is to be comforted for not having a full life. As he once wanted to be picked up and held when he skinned his knee, he now wants someone to console him for his lack of a life. But we are not talking about a skinned knee here; we are not talking about not *having* a life; we are talking about a life that is not being *lived*. Only in living his own full life will he free himself of his need to be consoled. Only then will he be able to tolerate solitude without fear, to be close to someone without overburdening and being let down by the relationship.

"You cannot be somebody's helpless child again, and you wouldn't be happy if you could," I tell him. "In fact, if your wish to be taken care of came true, you would probably be in a wheelchair. But you do not have to be a self-sufficient grown-up either. You can be a child of God, a child of life itself. You will discover something that underlies everything, which you can trust to uphold, guide, and fulfill you. It will even provide you with the loving companionship you need."

As I talk, Tom puffs and sighs repeatedly. "This sounds like what I have been needing," he says.

Human Life as Spiritual Awakening

The central idea of *Coming to Life* is that human development is essentially spiritual development and that its ultimate stage is not adulthood, but spiritual awakening. Even if some capabilities decline in later years, there can still be continued spiritual growth. Beyond and beneath our physical, sexual, emotional, and intellectual development is a continuing spiritual maturation. It is not a changing, but an awakening. In spiritual awakening dreams of self-completion are replaced with awareness of our individual oneness with the whole. This is not a time to be coped with, but to be welcomed—not all that's left when everything else goes, but rather what life builds to, its culmination. As the apple is most beautiful just before it drops from the tree and yields itself to the ground, so it is the spiritually mature, awakened individual who, having yielded self to life, is most beautiful, peaceful, wise, and, above all, loving.

Coming to Life is predicated on the idea that there is a universal underlying force that can prevail as harmony, love, peace, joy, freedom, and fulfillment—insofar as we are aligned with it. A companion premise is that particular problems bring to light particular ways in which we are misaligned, and are thus excellent guides in our quest for alignment. Ancient declarations of a fundamental order or mind and the hazards of opposing oneself to it are found in most contemplative branches of the world's great religions. In the East, the *Tao te Ching*, the *Bhagavad Gita*, and the *Upanishads* are some of the great scriptures that provide such guidance. And for those who grow up in Western culture, there is no more inspired written guidance than our own familiar Bible, when it is read in the light of everyday living.

But, for each of us, the most important articulations of truth are found in daily life. Considered together, ancient truths and firsthand experience are like two wires in a lightbulb between which the filament gives off light. When such a light goes on in us, we no longer grope or believe; we see. In such enlightened moments, not only are our own life burdens lightened, but we become ourselves living lights for others to see by. What is seen is a universal underlying force: God. What happens is full, real being—being that is blessed by seeing things in a true light. When we do not see things in a true light, our lives are cursed by our confusion. When we do see from a true perspective, our lives are blessed by that clarity. In this sense seeing *is* being, and we are primarily and ultimately seeing beings.

Some say, "Sorry, I just don't believe in God." But usually the God they don't believe in is one I don't believe in either. Besides, I don't *believe in* God any more than I believe in the law of gravity. I don't have to believe in gravity because I can count on it. When I depend on it (and not on anything else), it does not let me down. So God is not a question of belief, but of verifiable mind, order, law, and force. Because this force is universal, it applies to everyone and can be seen as reliable by anyone who relies on it. The more I am aligned with this fundamental force, the less I am hurt, and the more I can walk upright—safely, freely, and joyfully.

Often instead of "God" I have used the term *Fundamental Mind* to make clear that we are not talking about some fickle mind-in-space but rather a reality underlying everything. Other religions call it the Secret One, Self, Buddha, One Mind, the Unnameable. The most familiar name for this is *God*, but *Order of Being* or *Higher Power* are acceptable translations. When I feel like a motherless child and need to be reminded that I am loved and cared for, I pray to God. When I feel victimized and need to remember that the basis of my suffering is my ignorant violation of laws of being, I center on Fundamental Mind. The ancient Hebrews said it in their great Shema: "Hear O Israel, the Lord our God, the Lord is one."[1] "Not with our ancestors did the Lord make this covenant, but with us who are all of us here alive this day."[2] Seng T'san, the Buddhist sage, said, "When direct identification is sought, we can only say, 'Not two.'"[3] Jesus said it this way: "I and the Father are one."[4]

So, as the title implies, this is not a book about changing but about waking up to one's life. When we wake, what we wanted to change shrinks or disappears altogether. We can protect a child somewhat from bumps and bruises while she learns to walk, but in the long run her real safety does not come by protecting her from the law of gravity, but through her becoming one with it. Thenceforth it protects, upholds, and frees her. She transcends surface bumps and bruises by becoming aware of her oneness with a deep, invisible force. Something within her comes to and recognizes, *Ah, yes!* **This** *is it!* **Here** *it is.* **Now** *I see!* So she walks and runs and leaves bumps and bruises—even their memory— in her cloud of dust. In the same way even past bitterness, guilt, and hurt regarding others can disappear from our lives, first from experience and eventually even from memory, as we become properly oriented and aligned.

Toward True Oneness

My book *Whole Child/Whole Parent* considered the fact that parenthood is just as much a time of growing as childhood. *Coming to Life* may find us a bit disillusioned with our adult lives. This is not an age issue: Whether we are anxious teenagers, middle- aged and in mid-life crisis, or ninety and near death, disenchant- ment with ourselves and our lives comes and perhaps goes, only to come again. But our disillusionment moves us along in what can turn out to be a marvelous spiritual journey. The journey starts in separate personhood, which, though we do not know it, is largely a dream state. Collectively we dream we are isolated minds-in-bodies, who must either look after ourselves or find someone else to take over. Raised from childish dependency to- ward a goal of adult self-sufficiency, some suffer from never feel- ing sufficiently self-sufficient; others feel self-sufficient but "lonely at the top" or anxious about what's next. Increasingly we see it is impossible to be so "on our own." It is not only loneliness that troubles us, but the lurking sense that as separate selves we cannot last. Survival is our prevailing concern, and we shall see how it is manifest in an endless striving for oneness with something beyond ourselves.

What we imagined as children to be grown-up turns out, when we get there, to be maximum separateness. As feelings of separateness build, desire for oneness increases. But the quest for oneness diverges in two directions, one false and one true. In the false direction we cope with separateness by trying to establish a variety of supportive interpersonal connections. This connection-making agenda is our primary occupation and the cause of most troubles. Almost all compulsive behavior can be understood in terms of our quest for interpersonal connections of one sort or another. Almost all problems, big and small, can be understood in terms of such failing or yearned-for *interpersonal* connections. *Coming to Life* may find us at the end of our interpersonal tethers. When our interpersonal connections are taut, frayed, constricting, or broken, we are almost willing to consider an alternative perspective. Almost.

In contrast to the interpersonal connection-*making* approach to separateness is connection-*seeing* or *spiritual oneness*. "Spiritual" indicates that the primary issue in achieving this oneness is perceptual rather than physical, strategic, or interpersonal. Conscious spiritual oneness is the ultimate stage of human development and fulfillment.

What about love? If we relinquish our interpersonal connections, will our lives be lonely and loveless? If Tom begins to live his adult life and gives up his quest for someone to cling to, will he be alone? Certainly not. To walk, the child must first let go of his parent's hand. It may seem a fearsome severing of a love-connection. But once he discovers his oneness with the hidden forces and can walk and run and dance, he can share these joys with others, without constraint and without harm. If Tom learns to trust the force and source of his life beyond self and other, and thereby live up to his potential, he will also at last be able to participate in healthy, truly loving, even intimate relationships.

In spiritual consciousness love burgeons as the sharing of one-ness. Loneliness and conflict are eased; shared love and joy abound as we move from the long struggle to get love from each other toward the joy of being in love together. Love is the ulti-mate outcome of spiritual awakening.

Our yearning for love is entirely legitimate. To know ourselves to be loved, to become truly loving, and ultimately to *be in love with* each other is the fruit of highest understanding. But such loving oneness with each other depends on our individual con-scious oneness with the whole. In the meantime it is precise-ly our experiences of imperfect love that drive us toward the perfect. We tend to dismiss the troublesome side of our lives as either humdrum or hardship. But it is holy humdrum and holy hardship. Every problem has the potential to guide us toward love.

A woman I know lamented that life with her second husband is even worse than it was with the man she divorced. She is a mathematician, so I pointed out an odd discrepancy. If someone presents her with a very difficult math problem, she says, "Oh, wonderful! This is going to be really challenging!" But when her marriage proved difficult, she felt all worried and sorry for her-self, because for some reason she thought it wasn't supposed to be difficult.

It is best to look at problems as gifts to be unwrapped. That is what they are, and they never stop coming. There never comes a time of such mastery that life becomes a vacation resort we can lounge around in. But, from a spiritual perspective, problems become appreciable. No thornless bed of roses is promised, but the blossoming of a meaningful, fulfilling, and beneficial life is guaranteed. There is no success or failure here. The goal is not pleasure or power or even freedom from problems. We don't belong in a course we have already mastered; if we still have some problems, we must still have some business being alive.

It is a comforting trip, if not an entirely comfortable one. When we examine our lives in terms of these interpersonal connecting versus spiritual "one-ing" ways of being, we find that some of the tempests in our teapots were more legitimate and important than we thought. This helps us to stop beating on ourselves. At the same time we see that some terrible evils are, after all, meaningful gateways and skylights to enlightenment, healing, and transcendence. This helps us to stop feeling so sorry for ourselves and beating on God.

The question arises, "Whom can I trust? This book? This author?" No need to trust either. You can judge for yourself what is so and what is not. In the end you are your own best guru—your *life* is your guru. As you need them, special individuals may appear to help you find the road that leads to the road. But these are not your only teachers. Everything that happens to you is your teacher. The secret is to learn to sit at the feet of your own life and be taught by it. The more I come to see this, the more I am amazed by the way that I am being (and, though I didn't always see it, have always been) taught and brought along toward conscious oneness, loved along—to the whole by the whole, to God by God.

The first step in finding your way somewhere is to discover where you are to begin with. So ask yourself now, "On what road that leads to the road am I?" As you go through the next days, in solitary moments and when you are with others, begin to notice what is uppermost in your mind. Ask yourself these questions: "Where am I *always* coming from? What am I *always* driving at?" If you want to find your way from one state to another, you have to know what state you are in.

So for now travel with me on this journey by train of thought. Look out the window of your soul and see for yourself how the light strikes the ground—from your particular vantage point, at this now and that here. I wish you a pleasant journey, a bon voyage, a good seeing.

2. Dying to Wake Up

Without willing it I had gone from being ignorant of being ignorant to being aware of being aware. And the worst part of my awareness was that I didn't know what I was aware of, but I was certain that the things I had yet to be aware of wouldn't be taught to me at George Washington High School.

MAYA ANGELOU

Sometimes we know for a fact that "all's right with the world." Occasionally we see life as God is said to have seen it: *that it was good*. We have sat at some task or walked some path and seen ourselves as God is said to have seen us: *that it was very good*. In some moments of solitude we are filled with joy, energy, confidence, enthusiasm, and at the same time, peace of mind. In other moments we laugh, marveling at the good of seeing and being together. We say we are "in tune" or "in love," and indeed we are.

Everyone has such glimpses. As children we often had them. Now, having had some struggles, sometimes we experience sadness in these moments because the spaces between have turned joy into yearning. We aren't sure what makes them come or go, or how to make them stay. So we are wistful. But this is because we know what's good and true and *possible*. We are like straggly plants drawn toward the light. As Augustine recognized, "Our hearts are restless until they find their rest in thee."

We can't remember when we got our particular idea of "the goal." We may not even be able to say what it is. But for years we have climbed toward it. Our goal is a mixture of truth and illusion. Our valid underlying yearning for individual fulfillment and love is overlaid with a confused false interpersonal version of proving ourselves to others, at others' expense. We must relinquish this false goal before we can embrace the underlying valid one.

The point at which we begin to question our particular goal

varies for each of us. At what point this questioning pushes us onto the spiritual path differs. For most it happens repeatedly. Tripping, we stumble onto the path. Tripping again, we stumble off. Off and on. On and off. Young and restless, midway and unsure, dying or grieving and afraid. Said one individual on his deathbed, "The doctors have done everything they know how to do. They say I will die soon, but I keep thinking I could *know* something that could help. God doesn't seem real, but there must be something more. Otherwise it doesn't make sense."

Said another individual in an initial counseling session, "I have everything anyone could wish, but I just can't get going in the morning. I know I should be happy. There's nothing really wrong, but I don't find enough meaning to life. There must be something more—a better way of looking at things."

What do these people have in common? Both seek a new perspective. One prays for the first time in years; the other considers seeking help. Both have conceived of something beyond everything they have thought of so far—not something to do or get, but a new way of seeing. The mind opens. Each recognizes the need; each is open to the possibility; each is on the brink of something wonderful.

If your mind has opened in this way, then you are on the brink of something wonderful. Whether your problems are monumental or trivial, your entry to the spiritual path is equally legitimate and timely. The fact is that transcendence of the trivial is a step toward transcending the monumental. To set aside the day's affairs and let go into a night's sleep is a step toward setting aside the cares of this life to die happily. Of course, death comes to all and—in disappointment, loss, rejection, failure—we face many deaths before we die. So it is not a question of whether or not we die. It is a question of whether we live and will die struggling or, possibly, peacefully, gracefully, gratefully, and full of love.

"My, how foolish I am!" my friend cries, suddenly alert, like a woman remembering too late she has biscuits in the oven. "You know what I've always thought?" she asks in a tone of discovery, and not smiling at me but at a point beyond. "I've always thought a body would have to be sick and dying before they saw the Lord. And I imagined that when He came it would be like looking at the Baptist window: pretty as colored glass with the sun pouring through, such a shine you don't know it's getting dark. And it's been a comfort to think of that shine taking away all the spooky feeling. But I'll wager that it never happens. I'll wager at the very end a body realizes the Lord has already shown Himself. That things as they are"—her hand circles in a gesture that gathers clouds and kites and grass and Queenie pawing earth over her bone—"just what they've always seen was seeing Him. As for me, I could leave the world with today in my eyes."[1]

It used to be that psychiatry (which is about minds) and God (which is about one mind) didn't mix. But these days a book by a God-centered psychiatrist can break records. The road less traveled has gotten almost crowded. Anyone likely to read (or write) *Coming to Life* has enough to know that having enough isn't enough. Individually and collectively we have grown increasingly aware of this. We can have wonderful families and still be in hate, be surrounded by peace and still tremble, succeed in work and still fail, live in beautiful surroundings and still feel out of place. We know that happiness does not depend on circumstance, on what we are doing, or on what we have or where we have it, even with whom—but on our perspective. We sense there is something we're just not *seeing*, so we seek better mental and spiritual health. We associate happiness with something in thought. Like dreamers beginning to suspect it is "only a dream," more and more when faced with trouble we question our perspective. Like the bear who went over the mountain, business executives climb to the top only to see the other side. "Now what?" they ask. Or they have a heart attack and have to "take stock." Priorities shift. Perspectives change. The time comes, and now is.

Becoming Aware of Being Asleep

The first step toward seeing is becoming aware of not seeing— or at least of not seeing straight. The goal has to be questioned. For instance, it seems logical that whenever we feel bad, we seek to feel good; but sometimes we seek *bad* to feel good! We pay money for terrifying entertainment, love a good cry, get a bang out of life-threatening sport, sleep away our one free day, shy from opportunity, itch to fight, work ourselves to death, and even while pacing the waiting rooms of cancer wards, we say, "I'm dying for a smoke." Occasionally the question crosses our minds—Why am I doing this? Why don't I stop?

Even good dreams of happiness turn out to have been misguided. So in *Gulliver's Travels* it is said that, "God has discovered that the best way to punish a man for his sins is to give him too much of what he wants." An oriental curse seethes, "May you get what you want." Emerson warned, "Beware of what you set your heart on, for you may get it." Teresa of Avila observed that "More tears have been shed over answered than over unanswered prayers." From folk myth to sage wisdom, we hear that major goals often turn into main pains.

Your main pain may come suddenly or have been there all along. To avoid it you have probably limited yourself in some way, hanging back or hanging on *lest* . . . it may come as a huge, upsetting, life-altering event or just a nagging fear—the target you most wish to avoid hitting. Typical main pains center around major fears such as not to be alone, never to be rejected or criticized; and around cherished goals—*the* goal—such as always to be respected, accepted, liked, taken care of, thought strong, creative, in control, nice.

Main pains are what we most wish but feel least able to do something about. Of them we say *if only*. If only it weren't for this, everything would be all right. If only that won't or will happen. If only he—if only she—. Whether as worst-fears-come-true or heart's-desires-that-won't, main pains can overshadow and ruin everything. One man reported:

When I was young and single I thought, *This would probably be the most wonderful time in my life if only I knew that eventually I would get married— that I wouldn't be alone forever.* But I couldn't know that, so instead of being footloose and fancy free I forced myself to go to singles bars, which I hated, in search of the girl of my dreams, which I wasn't dreaming yet.

There are three phases of main pain: (1) being unable to get what we want; (2) getting what we thought we wanted but it isn't working out right, or having what we want and it is working out but we fear to lose it; and (3) losing it and wanting it all over again.

Whenever our main pain is acute, we are disturbed. We can't keep our mind on our work (or stop working), can't eat (or stop eating), can't sleep (or stop sleeping), can't sit still (or lift a finger). At such times many are sure that there is something very wrong with them; others are overwhelmed with the feeling that life is meaningless.

Whatever our false surface goal may be, before it can be relinquished, it has to be questioned. Before it can be questioned, it has to become questionable. For most of us this is a painful process. For anything cherished to become questionable it has to not work out. We may have to be hurt many times before we can question our wish. This process of our false goal proving itself false to us is painful, but it is also good. The false proving itself false is just the dark side of the truth proving itself true.

As the thought *I could wake up now* is admitted when the dream becomes intolerable, these questions finally dawn on us. We question ourselves. How could this have happened? How could I have been so deluded? Why didn't I see? We question our living dreams turned living nightmares. Later we will recall that we have always heard these voices—questions, warnings. "Wait a minute. Are you sure? What's the rush? Wait and see." We heard, but pushed them down because of some supposed good we "had" to have. Some day we will recognize these voices as one voice, the same still small voice that the prophet Elijah heard as he hid in the mountains, when he was at the end of his rope—and scared to death:

And, behold, the Lord passed by, and a great and strong wind rent the mountains, and broke in pieces the rocks before the Lord, but the Lord was not in the wind; and after the wind an earthquake, but the Lord was not in the earthquake; and after the earthquake a fire, but the Lord was not in the fire; and after the fire a still small voice.[2]

The voice is not in the wind or earthquake or fire; but it isn't until after wind, quake, and fire that most of us are ready to listen.

Persistent Variations on a Troublesome Theme

The good news is that you aren't the only one. I confess I am still heartened by every student tale that reminds me that, one way or another, "everybody's got something"—that I'm not the only one. The bad news is that main pains are chronic. In my weekly seminars members present ordinary difficulties for consideration in a spiritual light. These are not encounter groups. We do not talk about how we feel about each other. Instead we tell each other stories, baffling little anecdotes from firsthand experience, and then we look at them in a spiritual light. We try to see what ideas are running our lives. Then we look for truer, spiritual ideas and consider how to let them take charge of us. But whether recounting one's own experience or interpreting another's, there is a commonality to each person's presentation. It's almost like a chamber music group. We have cellos, violas, and violins—each with its own theme, each rendering the theme of the day in its own unique way. A pitch for admiration, a plea for sympathy—we each have a theme song, our own "The Me" song. It is often only after recognizing the thematic character of others' problems that we begin to recognize the mental basis of our own difficulties—an important step in spiritual growth and healing.

The suspicion that we aren't seeing straight is the beginning of seeing straight. We may begin by noticing a pattern in our lives. Others have other difficulties. Hauntingly our particular difficulty persists—no matter how we try to change our experience, no matter how we try to change ourselves. *Oh, no! Not that again! This is just what I was trying to avoid! I was sure this time would be different. I was sure I had changed.* A new job, a new relationship, but the same old problem.

In a first session a young woman told of two devastating romances in two years. She could see too many similarities between the men in these relationships. She wanted to know what made her fall in love with the same type of person. "I think maybe I sort of ask for it," she said. "They say things happen in threes—but twice is enough for me!" She was on the right track for sure, and I could reassure her that as bad as she felt at the time, if she was waking to this after only two years and only two romances, she had a lot to be grateful for. Most take longer.

"After eighteen years in a miserable marriage I finally got divorced," said one man. "I thought I would never fall in love again, but I did. She seemed completely different from my first wife. We married, and I was so happy. But in less than a year it has all turned sour. She's doing the same things to me—even worse. How could I have been so deceived?" He wanted to know what to do about his wife. When I suggested that she was not his problem, that it would be more helpful to look at what attracted him to such experiences, he was outraged.

"You mean it's me?" he said. "No, I can't accept that . . . I didn't do anything to deserve that kind of treatment."

"Who proposed the marriage?" I asked.

"I did. Oh!"

His wife was not the cause of the problem, but neither was he. There was just a mistaken idea about life and love that they both had. They made a deal around that idea, and because it was a lousy idea, it worked out to be a lousy deal.

"And if I don't face the idea, it could happen again?" he asked.

"Yes," I answered. "But on the other hand whatever this idea is, it has already been hurting you for a very long time. If you get free of your troublesome idea now, this could be the beginning of its never hurting you again."

The dynamics of life experience are very like dreaming. In dreams, too, it is necessary to recognize from some other viewpoint than that of ourselves in the dream *that* we are dreaming. As a child I repeatedly dreamed that the ground was falling from under my feet. I saw the clifflike sides of an ever-widening abyss as I ran, desperately trying to stay atop the crumbling earth. The frightening dream always woke me, but it seemed so real that even after I woke up enough to open my eyes I did not dare to close them again, because immediately the horrible vision would continue. Yet even mid-dream there was always a rational background awareness that if the ground really were crumbling, no amount of running would keep me up. The special agony of the dream was this thought that since running couldn't work, the experience must not be real and was therefore somehow self-inflicted—that if only I dared to stop running, the earth would stop crumbling. A lifetime later I recognize this as the still small voice of truth reaching into my nightmares, inviting me to wake up. We are never allowed to be completely convinced of our own suffering. Mercy!

In life, as in dreams, I have seen that my perception precedes not only my experience of what happens, but even what happens. There is always this voice that points to my responsibility. "There is a lesson to learn here," it says, "or a blessing to be recognized." In life, as in my dream, such guidance has always been quietly available in the background. Though it tells me things I do not want to hear, I appreciate that it never gives up on me. It suggests that I am not abandoned. No matter what my predicament, it is always there. "Whither shall I flee from thy spirit? . . . If I make my bed in Hell, even there shalt thou find me."[3]

There is something that loves us, something bigger to which we belong that holds us to itself even as we writhe in restless sleep. We are as numb fingers prickling, able to move and function somewhat, yet not fully alive and whole. So we yearn to be fully awake. Or is it God yearning, as we yearn for the feeling in numbed parts to return? Does Fundamental Mind yearn for us to awaken to life as necessary, beloved aspects of its own self? I think so.

You are approaching the possibility of waking up when you ask, *Why is this thing that is so easy for others so hard for me? How do I invite this—the same experience happening over and over? What is there for me to learn here?* If you suspect your mindset, if you do not want to keep helplessly repeating the same mistakes, if you do not want to keep being needlessly upset—then you are getting ready to wake up. There must be more to life than just not being upset. Some go right on blaming others. Some don't. What is one person's lame excuse is another's valued opportunity. One brother grew up to be a homeless alcoholic bum, the other a happily married, highly successful businessman. Each was asked, privately and individually, to explain himself. The bum threw up his hands helplessly. "My father was an alcoholic," he said. "Well, you see," explained his brother cheerfully, "my father was an alcoholic."

Sometimes we blame others too much, sometimes we blame ourselves. Since both tendencies interfere with our being awake and responsive to life, ultimately both have to be outgrown. But it is initially positive when we look to ourselves for the determining factors in our experience.

The twice-married man returns. "You say it isn't her fault. I find that hard to accept because then I think you mean it is my fault. Yet you say it isn't my fault either."

"Right. There is just some mistaken idea on which you are both relying. It is letting you both down by crumbling under the weight of your reliance."

"Could you please tell me what my mistaken idea is?"

The immediate benefit of such receptivity is that you are no longer a victim. Once your life is in your lap, then so is the possibility of improving it! How much more hopeful and reasonable this is than the idea that the world has to be changed.

Where Do We Get Off?

Two men, one occidental and one oriental, were taking a computer course. After several hours of tedious programming the oriental mentioned that he couldn't get his program to work. Thinking he recognized the problem, the occidental suggested that he type in a certain command. The oriental did so, but then instead of working, his program disappeared entirely from the computer's memory. The occidental, appalled and sorry, apologized profusely. But the oriental smiled broadly in genuine grat-itude. "Don't be sorry," he said brightly. "I'm very glad! Now I know: *Never do that!*"

This ability to respond gratefully to problems as a learner is one of the first signs of spiritual awakening. At first we just want to stop the pain. But our pain is teaching us something, bringing us somewhere. Occasionally you meet an individual who, sud-denly confined to a wheelchair or facing premature death, ex-presses gratitude for something his predicament has forced him to see. He tells how shallow his life was before his accident jolted him. His face is radiant, full of peace, joy, compassion. When he laughs, you hear that he knows something. When you look into his eyes, you see that he has seen something. When you first meet such people, you feel horrified by what they lack, but you leave wondering if you will ever see what they have seen.

Reluctant though we are to give up self-pity or righteous in-dignation, our questions begin to shift from "What can I do?" and "How can I feel better?" to "What do I need to see?" This question is a turnstile into the spiritual way, where blame and battle and fair and unfair simply no longer apply, where humility and learning begin, where the joy of discovery and growth takes place. Are we no longer content to blame something or someone outside of ourselves? Are we no longer convinced that either the problem or the answer lie completely within our own power? If so, we are in remarkably good company.

Behind every great religion stood a great teacher. As different as they were from each other, there is one thing in which they were the same. They all identified flawed perception as our fun-damental difficulty:

For as he thinketh in his heart, so is he.[4]

> We are what we think,
> having become what we thought.
> Like the wheel that follows the cart-pulling ox,
> sorrow follows an evil thought.

And joy follows a pure thought,
like a shadow faithfully tailing a man.
We are what we think,
having become what we thought.[5]

Only so few—Jesus, Buddha, Lao Tsu, and some followers—have stood on this frontier before. But now their idea that suffering can be approached perceptually is more widely considered. More and more we respond to problems by looking for a truer *perspective*.

If you are seeking better *mental* health and peace of *mind*, it is because something in you will not settle for less than to understand, will not tolerate less than to be loving, cannot accept the bad with the good, or abide a "reality" that is not perfect. You suspect what the wise knew. They too were once disturbed. They could not settle for what you cannot settle for either. So perhaps you, too, can hope to see what they saw that made them fearless, peaceful, loving, and beneficial.

Embarking earnestly on her own spiritual awakening, a lovely college student questioned her right to pursue these ideas while so many others suffer from poverty and hunger.

"Isn't it self-centered for me just to work on my own peace while the whole Third World is starving?" she said.

"Why does a plant bloom?"

"For itself, I guess. That's its life," said the student.

"Yes, but what good is the blossom?"

Surely it is for its own good that the plant struggles to flower, but we know that there are much larger forces that bring it into bloom and that its blooming is for a greater good. Neither are we turning our back on the world's darkness when we seek an inner light. After all, the same madness that produces world wars, starving millions, and refugee children is what also produces strife in families. Can we possibly hope to abolish global terrorism, famine, and injustice before we can give up arguing at dinner and fighting over who's got the most blanket and should do which chores? We have tried to do better; what we need is to see better. So now let's see. Life bullies us along; our spiritual leaders beckon; an inner voice already whispers: *Let's see. Let's see now.*

It is not easy. It is a struggle. In a dark corner an onion in an onion bin begins to sprout. Pale, thin, and twisted the sprout grows, stretching and straining for the light. Roots spring forth, feeling all over for water and food. Is it trying so hard? Yes and no. We know that the onion sprout, too, is drawn by the sun, that the onion is driven and drawn by a life urge and source far beyond itself. And so it is with us. And this is called grace.

For those in quest of spiritual awakening, this knowledge of grace is the blessing. There still is suffering, but now it is meaningful. Where formerly we had the sense of being hurt and punished for nothing, now we have a suspicion growing into a conviction that we are being lovingly guided and set free by a somehow familiar gentle giant, the wondrous whole to which we belong. This makes it easier to learn and be guided by life. It makes everything easier and better. The prophet Hosea saw this. He envisioned God as a loving parent, trying to rescue and protect his children, restraining them where possible from injury, comforting them compassionately when in ignorance they hurt themselves. Hosea saw their suffering as arising from their pulling away, like children struggling in their parents' arms, from a God who nevertheless always had and always would hold them close and keep them safe. Hosea heard God saying,

> When Israel was a child, I loved him
> and out of Egypt I called my son.
> The more I called them,
> the more they went from me;
> they kept sacrificing to the Ba-als
> and burning incense to idols.
>
> Yet it was I who taught Ephraim to walk,
> I took them up in my arms,
> but they did not know that I healed them.
> I led them with cords of compassion,
> with bands of love,
> and I became to them as one

who eases the yoke on their jaws,
and I bent down to them and fed them.[6]

As each of us wakes up, the whole world wakes up a little. It is as if we were in a dark, windowless barn. Blind and up against a wall, we struggle to move along, stumbling over and hurting each other in the process. But every now and then, feeling along the wall, one of us comes to a corner and discovers another wall. He or she, whoever it may be, feels along that wall, comes to a door, opens it, and is confronted at last by a much larger, brighter space where he finds he can see. As he stands in the doorway, the rest of us see the light on him. When he steps outside, we wonder where he has gone. Now by the light shining through the empty doorway we find our way as well. Others have gone through the door for us. Each of us goes through the door for others.

3. Is There Life Beyond Coping?

Trying to control the future
Is like trying to take the Master Carpenter's place.
When you handle the Master Carpenter's tools,
chances are that you'll cut your hand.

LAO TZU

Under hypnosis a woman was instructed that soon after being awakened she would open and close her umbrella. Sure enough, she rose from her chair, crossed the room, picked up her umbrella, opened and closed it, put it down, and returned to her seat as if nothing had happened. Questioned as to why she had done this, she explained, "I just wanted to see if it was working." But why now, in the middle of a conversation? "Well, isn't it better to make sure that it works now than to wait until I get out in the rain to find out that it's broken?" she replied testily. Actually she had no idea why she had opened the umbrella because the suggestion had been made in her sleep, yet she felt compelled to make up a rationalization for having done so, and, in some fear, to defend it.

In this way she revealed the presence of a second hypnotic suggestion: that it is extremely important never to look stupid, always to appear rational to others, that this is the goal. She was not aware of where this strong impulse had come from either, because it, too, had been suggested to her in her sleep—the dream of childhood. She had no choice but to carry out these ideas, because she had no idea that they were only ideas, not necessarily founded in reality, not necessarily a matter of life and death. So she struggled to appear in control, while ideas she didn't even know she had were in complete charge of her.

Day by day, year after year, we live our lives out of certain fundamental assumptions of which we are almost completely unaware. These assumptions govern our lives, yet they are so universal and unquestioned as to be virtually unconscious. We can discover our assumptions by examining our behavior. If you tickle a friend with a blade of grass from behind, you can see from the way she swats her neck that she believes an insect is trying to get at her. Her behavior reveals her perspective. This chapter is about some of our habitual behavior, our knee-jerk reactions to life. By looking at our behavior and our language we can discover some of our underlying beliefs. They are very strong convictions about staying alive, but some of them are mistaken and are killing us.

A Sense of Separation

If we are looking for something, clearly we don't think we have it. So if we are looking for peace of mind, security, love, fulfillment, these must be qualities we think we lack. But exactly what do we think is lacking? Our language is revealing. If we are slightly upset, we say we feel "at loose ends," "out of it," "frayed," "a bit off," "falling apart." If someone is crazy, he is "unstrung," "really off," "unhinged," "undone," has "lost his grip," or is "out of touch with reality." These terms are remarkably similar to our language for death. In dying we "hang on by a thread," "slip away," or "let go" of life. Death is a "parting," a "going away," the ultimate "separation." Someone who dies has been "taken from us" and we are "left behind." We feel the loss of someone "to hang onto," the breaking of an important "tie." We feel "cut off," "adrift," "alone," "lonely," "apart," and "broken up."

Our language suggests that we perceive separateness, death, and upset to be almost synonymous. Separateness disturbs us and makes us act in more or less crazy ways. I don't know about you, but I just want to be loved. If people don't love me, I feel afraid, as if my life were in danger. It doesn't take a gunshot wound, just someone looking away. So I spend half my time trying to do things that I hope will make people love me; I spend the other half avoiding everything I think will make them reject me. This is crazy—and worse. But what looks insane on the outside may be quite reasonable from the inside. On a talk show a man recovering from manic/depressive psychosis was asked if he could recall the perception that so disturbed him. He answered without hesitation. "I felt so completely isolated and apart from everyone else—so completely alone."

We do not have to look to psychiatric wards for examples. From childish "separation anxiety" to our own "sense of isolation," we are bothered by separateness. It shows in our ambivalence about being together. We find it hard to get along, but intolerable to be apart. As relieved as we are when a houseguest goes, we are eager to see the next one come. "I need some peace and quiet. I want to get away from it all. I have to get some time to myself," we complain. Yet when privacy is possible, we often avoid it. Even after a hectic week with hordes of people and no leisure, many become anxious or depressed when confronted with long-sought solitude. "I had the whole day off, but I just wasted it!" A vacation, a free day, an hour or two when the kids are at school gets filled with a flurry of phone calls to "get in touch," to arrange a "get together." A character in the movie *Four Seasons* says, "You know what the ties are that bind us together? Fear and panic."

Fear and panic about what? We have no common name for it—or only vague ones like restlessness, anxiety, blues. Small words for such a universal experience. We have no precise name because we do not understand it. We do not understand because we have not faced it. Whenever it surfaces, we quickly bury or get rid of it. One man reported:

I realize I have a whole repertoire that I run through. Call someone. Switch on the television or radio. Drink, eat, or buy something. Masturbate. Daydream. Sleep. I have an enormous repertoire of ways to avoid confronting whatever it is. I'm not sure what I think will happen—

but there is some sort of fear in the background. I think it has to do with feeling alone.

Repertoires

We all have repertoires. There are three levels to our repertoires, each with a whole spectrum of options. What is important to recognize is that they all involve us in making contact with someone or something else. First choice for most is to get in touch with other *persons*—a friend, a committee, an impromptu "get together," a sudden impulse to call an old friend and "renew an old tie."

Second, if we cannot make "meaningful contact" with people, we reach for *things*—a bite, a sip, a smoke, a project, a projection. Scores of people who have everything shop endlessly for gimmicks, "notions," and irresistible bargains. Whole departments thrive on such "impulse" purchases. But what is the impulse? Others cruise car showrooms, or shops full of power tools. Buyers groan under sixteen tons of "high interest" payments. Why? Underlying this perpetual shopping is some anxiety that is briefly relieved when contact is made in the form of a purchase.

The third level is "getting in touch with my *self*." Small children do it unabashedly in public, one hand in mouth, the other either wrapped around head to twiddle with hair or ear, or stuck in pants to fiddle with more private parts. Adults do this more discreetly—masturbating in private, fussing over blemishes, brows, bulges, and bald spots. When we can't count on others to help us handle life, we handle ourselves.

Most people rank the routines in their repertoires in descending order of preference: people, thing, self. They like it best if a sort of club sandwich of all levels can be assembled, as when two friends meet at a fine department store to discuss spouses and purchases over lunch. Business people gather to golf, confer, fish, and soak up sun in the Bahamas, plugging into each other, pulling strings, and tying up loose ends. Fathers who miss their families all week crouch together in dark rooms on sunny Saturdays, drinking beer, watching ball, telling dirty jokes. Children's faces shine in at the door. Their voices tinkle like wind chimes.

"Is it almost over, Dad? Soon can we play?"

"Later. We're busy," they say. "Not now. Go away."

When one routine gets us nowhere, we swiftly swerve into others. When our own life dead ends, we turn to the vicarious: "Reach for that dial." Turn on what turns you on: a soap opera, a game show with costly prizes, a thriller, a "contact sport," a "touching drama." When good or healthy routines fail, we even turn to bad ones. There is a wide range of healthy and unhealthy activities on each level. While the merits of good over bad habits seem indisputable, often they are not. So diligence becomes workaholism, and doing good becomes patronizing.

On some level we suspect both "good" and "bad" behaviors, especially excesses—excessive involvements and excessive avoidances. We sense when our priorities aren't quite straight, when we don't put first things first, when we are not quite peaceful. We may not have a shameful habit. Perhaps we are even overly good, practically perfect—and yet if we are honest, we are not truly happy. We sense something is amiss.

I complimented a very community-minded individual on being such "a need meeter." "I'm not so sure," he reflected. "Am I a need meeter—or just a need needer?"

Erma Bombeck describes such a person:

Everyone said Sharon was a terrific mother. Her neighbors said it . . . Her mother said it . . . Her children's teacher said it . . . Her best friend said it . . .

Sharon kept a schedule that would have brought any other woman to her knees. Need twenty-five women to chaperone a party? Give the list to Sharon. Need a mother to convert the school library to the Dewey Decimal system? Call Sharon. Need someone to organize a block party, garage sale, or school festival? Get Sharon.

Sharon was a Super Mom!

Her gynecologist said it.

Her butcher said it.

Her tennis partner said it.

Her children . . .

Her children never said it.

They spent a lot of time with Rick's mother, who was always home and who ate cookies out of a box and played poker with them.[1]

Coping

Repertoires are ways we cope with life. Coping is part of our definition of being grown-up. It means having things under control, being able to "handle ourselves" in life. But what is coping? Coping is making the best of a bad situation. Isn't life more than a bad situation to be coped with? Isn't there more to life than coping? Isn't there more to us that cope-ability?

There comes an end to coping, a time (and times) when our main pain is acute and we aren't coping well at all. *I'll get over it, but right now I don't see how,* we say. *I just have to wait for it to pass.* From dim dissatisfaction to pure desperation, from minor mishap to major catastrophe, sooner or later everyone has both, and we cry out:

"I worked harder than anyone, but I was passed over again for promotion. It isn't fair."

"I meet girls all the time, but nothing comes of it. What's wrong with me? Why am I so alone?"

"It was my idea, but someone else got the credit. I built that business from scratch, and they just took over. Screwed by my best friend. I never should have trusted him."

"What if it's cancer?"

"They took off my leg!"

"So we finally sold our house and bought a retirement home, and now they say my wife has Alzheimer's."

"My wife! My son! I loved them best and hurt them most of all! I am so sorry! I am so ashamed!"

Even without disasters, the better we cope, the more we are aware of a dimension to life that we are not tapping into—a fullness, a richness. Good coping is not to be sneezed at. Some cope better than others. Most of us cope better than we used to, and coping is better than falling apart. But aren't we just coping too much of the time? Is there life beyond coping?

The Compulsion Factor

There is something fishy about so much coping. Behind mildly restless, merely inefficient, as well as desperate and dangerous ways of coping is a certain compulsion that we "gotta do something." There is a certain awareness that at least some of this effort is fruitless, even counterproductive. The apostle Paul lamented this when he said, "The good that I would I do not; and the evil that I would not, that I do."[2] From things we ought but can't bring ourselves to do, to things we ought not but can't resist doing, there is something strangely driven about our behavior. Coping may give us the feeling of "having a grip" on life and not losing control of ourselves, but a closer look reveals that there is something controlling us. Not only are we never quite peaceful, the fact is that we often shun peace. We are really driven in some sense all the time. What is this compulsion?

Alone and Afraid: Facing the Fear

To understand the compulsion behind coping repertoires we first need to understand what is being coped with. One moment you are doing something reasonable, next you have jumped tracks and gone off in some other direction. One moment you are present; next you are searching your repertoire for what will do the trick. What trick? Like a daddy longlegs tapping its antennae, we constantly feel for something. But what? What drives Sharon to be a Super Mom? What compels another to watch television all day while laundry and the sense of failure pile up? Why is Harry's basement full of power tools, his house in disrepair? What gets us going so? What holds us back like this? What is the common factor in all compulsive coping?

In an episode of television's *Star Trek* a highly evolved being of bodiless intelligence temporarily assumes human form. He reflects on being in a body again. "Hmm. Very interesting . . . so warm and exciting. So beautiful. But it is so lonely! I had forgotten how lonely it is!" We all have something in common with him, and with the man on the talk show who "felt so isolated and apart." Behind our repertoires we found compulsion. Behind compulsion we discover aloneness. Behind aloneness we come face to face with fear. When the sense of aloneness comes, if we do not immediately "do something," we are confronted with fear.

The onset of fear and the urge to reach out may come when there is no apparent danger. One woman had the secret thought that women were stupid and weak, and that men were smart and powerful. The main focus of her life was to destroy men's mental power and acquire it for herself. This quest took many forms—sexual, vocational, and academic. In her academic work she noticed an odd compulsion.

Whenever I try to study at home, I begin to eat compulsively. The only way to keep from doing this is to study in the library. Otherwise I would just keep getting fatter, and no studying would ever get done because I would just keep trotting back and forth to the kitchen.

For her, studying was loaded with extra meaning and importance. It was at once promising and threatening. Because of her belief that her life depended on her mind power, when she studied, she felt her life was at stake. To an ambitious individual the thought of academic failure is like the thought of dying. So when she studied, the thought that she might fail was extremely threatening. Eating was a way of fortifying herself, and, by not studying, she could not fail. If we are falling, it seems perfectly reasonable to reach out and grab onto something. Likewise seemingly unreasonable compulsions have underlying, compelling rationales. All compulsive behaviors make sense in relation to some perceived threat to self survival. It is impossible to give up the compulsive behavior until the underlying perception of threat is faced and seen to be false.

We are not concerned here with changing behavior, only with understanding it in order to discover the thoughts behind it, in order eventually to turn to a freeing understanding. The first step is to familiarize yourself with your own repertoire of compulsions. In the next few days take note of the things you habitually do that are not quite reasonable. Watch for small detours, quirky behavior, overindulgences, overreactions.

One man noticed that he couldn't stand to have his wife fall asleep beside him in the car. He was also unable to go to sleep at night if she went to sleep first. He felt compelled to keep her awake and, if she fell asleep, to wake her up—by clearing his throat, bumping into her, humming, and so on. When he couldn't keep her awake, he felt angry at her. When he refrained from acting upon his impulse to wake her, he noticed fear. "If she is away, I have no trouble going to sleep alone. If I am alone in the car, I am not a bit uncomfortable. But if she is beside me and asleep, I feel anxious." He couldn't stand to be ignored by her. Somehow he depended on her paying attention to him.

Next time a compelling urge comes, if you wait a minute before reaching for something, you may catch yourself feeling distinctly alone and afraid. Watch and see. First you want to do something; second, if you refrain from doing it, you begin to feel afraid. Try it. When some compulsion hits you, instead of immediately acting upon it, just wait. Abstain. Refrain. Suppose your impulse is to postpone something. Maybe you have even begun the job. You are nearly finished. There is plenty of time before your next appointment. Another half hour and you can check it off. Yet you find it harder to stick with it. You feel yourself pulling away. It may come as a desire to sleep, or eat, or just a growing restlessness that says, *What else can I do? Who can I call? Where else can I go?* Some people have the opposite compulsion of always being driven to do something, and never being able to relax. Whatever your version may be, if you do not immediately give in to it, you will discover next that it isn't just laziness or procrastination or even pleasure-seeking that has you going. Instead you are afraid.

Alone? So what? Afraid? Of what? Feel it. What is it? Fear and separateness. Separateness and fear. These occur together.

The longer you refrain from your compulsion, the bigger the fear. Keep waiting. Don't do it. Isn't it curious? Isn't it interesting? Now ask yourself, "What do I think will happen if I don't do this?" The answer is, nothing—at least nothing important. In some way that is what we are afraid of: nothing—of being nothing, of not being anything at all. We may believe that we don't think much about death, but the anxiety produced in this little experiment reveals that on some level we really do think about it. What we do as much as possible is to avoid thinking about it. It is not that we are suffocating. It is not that we are freezing or starving or bleeding or burning. We may be in perfectly good health, with plenty of air to breathe, in no immediate danger of dying whatsoever, yet we feel the need to fight or flee *as if for dear life*, and to grab onto almost anything *as if for life support*. Why? There is something unreasonable here. And there is something very reasonable here: We do not want *not* to be.

Existential Dread

The experience to which we have given little names like "restlessness" and "anxiety" is really a much bigger matter, which is why philosophers have given it much bigger names: "threat of annihilation," "fear of non-being," "existential dread," "fear of nothingness."

To understand what underlies your own compulsive coping behavior it helps to notice when it begins. Ask yourself, "Exactly what was the thought that preceded the thought to do this not quite reasonable thing?" See if a threatening thought does not come to mind. It may be only after a few hours or days when you notice you have been a little "off base," distracted, inclined to overindulge or overreact. But once you have caught yourself in the middle of your coping repertoire, if you ask yourself when it began, you remember what triggered it. Very likely it was something someone said or didn't say about you, did or did not think or do in your direction.

A threat to the life of the ego is like a threat to the life of the body. It does not have to be a fatal diagnosis. Just a hint of inadequacy or rejection will do. A comment from your spouse. "What have you done to your hair?" "Are you really planning to wear that tie?" A remark from your boss. "I've got my eye on Harry. He's showing real promise, don't you think?" A smile someone didn't return. A fantasy that crossed your mind ("What if I can't do this right? What if I can't do it in time? What if it's—what if I'm—not good enough? What if they don't like it? What if they don't like me?"). The threat is always of some separation—from job, boss, financial support, family, spouse, from psychological and emotional outreach and support—from whatever you see as your interpersonal life-support system.

Whatever it is, you felt threatened. You felt the life of your self threatened. You felt not worthy. Left out. Demeaned. Diminished. Called into question. Whenever something makes you doubt your viability, a desire to make some connection is triggered. Whatever the threat, it has mobilized you. Right now you've got to reach out for support from someone or something.

The impression of being one lone, insufficient being gives rise to a further impression of having to look out for ourselves. Immediately we start running into limitations. We are limited in what we know, have, can do, and whether and how long we can last. With the impression of being finite comes the experience of finitude—of both endedness and endability. We ask, *How am I doing? Am I doing? How am I? Am I? Or am I not?*

To understand the universality of this fear watch Stanley Kubrick's movie of Arthur C. Clarke's 2001 and pay particular attention to the space-walking scene. The astronaut emerges from the spaceship—a little bright thing on a string, floating in endless blackness. In one dreadful moment his umbilical cord to the "mother ship" is broken. Like an inflated, unbound balloon released, he spins crazily into space, fizzling into nothingness. One minute he is a brave, bright star. Next he is a meteorite bound for destruction. If we gasp with the rest, then we have not transcended the fear of annihilation. Our gasp means we believe that the worst thing is to be cut loose in space—that so separated we would be annihilated. We believe in the void. Not being self-sufficient, we infer that we must stay hooked up to something in order not to be annihilated by the void. If lots of people did not believe this, *2001* could not be such a success. If we did not believe it, we would not gasp.

2001 is a modern myth of archetypal significance. It is the story of human beings and space. Physically we survived after the umbilical cord was cut—to breathe and eat and walk by direct reliance on the environment. But psychologically we are afraid we will die if we let go of each other. We are sure there is nothing between us but nothing. Of course, *2001* also includes our hope, our suspicion that there is life beyond death, something beyond the nothing, because the next time we see the falling, dying, "lost in space" man, he has become an infant, no longer in a space suit, but in an amniotic sac, a baby about to be born. Just as birth gets us to death, so, perhaps we suspect, does dying get us to birth. It is something enormous to consider. Is it wishful thinking, or is there something real beyond it all that puts such ideas into our heads? Mythologist Joseph Campbell points out that universally the hero is one who dies to one context in order to be born to another:

We begin to see this incredible pattern of death giving rise to birth, and birth giving rise to death. . . . This is an essential experience of any mystical realization. You die to your flesh and are born into your spirit. You identify yourself with the consciousness and life of which your body is but the vehicle. You die to the vehicle and become identified in your consciousness with that of which the vehicle is the carrier. That is the God.[3]

Everyone faces heroic challenges of death and rebirth, not only at times of physical birth and death, but in everyday life. One woman had an unreasonable fear that her husband might die. Her fear was especially acute when he was on business trips. In counseling she saw that he was not her only source of protection or love. For the most part she was unusually assured, independent, skillful at managing her affairs and getting along with others. She was also independently wealthy. Nevertheless the fear persisted. One day in a counseling session she recognized the tendency of people literally to live off each other. She saw how parents use children to build images of themselves as parents, how heroes depend on the existence of victims, victims on victimizers. Suddenly she gave a startled sound. "So *that* is the meaning of my fear of my husband's death. If he dies, I will no longer be his wife." It was not only the loss of his life that she had feared, but of her life as his wife. Her fear was not of his dying but of her dying. She had not yet realized that her dying could also be her birthing. If she weren't connected to her husband, like astronaut to mother ship, perhaps she would become nothing. She did not yet see—but soon would—that there were dimensions of her life that she was dead to because of tethering herself to a person.

Compulsions arise from our natural desire to survive. No wonder some of our measures are so extreme; no wonder we expend such huge amounts of energy on our repertoires. We understand how even our little semi-acceptable ("I'm not hurting anyone but myself") habits have such a powerful hold, and why we have crazy thoughts ("I am *dying* for a new car." "I would *kill* for an invitation to that party.").

Coping is fine as far as it goes. It occurs at points where we think we are in danger of dying (and are not yet aware of the opportunity of birth). But it's really only a cover-up. There comes a time when the coping wears thin and gets a bald spot in it. The bald spot is growing, and no matter how carefully we comb long strands of coping across it—connecting this to that, me to it— the feared thing shows through and can't be covered up and has to be faced.

Coping is a waste of good anxiety. A better use of anxiety is to understand its meaning, question its basis, look for new possibility. Don't reject your anxiety. Accept it as part of the journey.

Recognize its legitimacy and its universality, and the worthy challenge it presents. It is not a flaw in rotten you, neither is it a dirty deal played by life on poor you. Once you have faced it squarely, you can forgive both yourself for worrying and life for worrying you. You can look behind the worry for both its basis *and* its baselessness. If its baselessness can be uncovered, then we can seek a better, truer premise on which to base our fuller lives. This is the best way to approach both death and life.

4. Yearning to Make Connections

The only true wisdom lies far from mankind, out in the great loneliness . . .

IGJUGARJUK, AN ESKIMO SHAMAN

Forgive, O, Lord, my little jokes on Thee
And I'll forgive Thy great big one on me.
ROBERT FROST

Suppose *you* are being tickled on the back of the neck with a blade of grass. Believing a mosquito is trying to bite you, you keep slapping your neck. Added to the fear of being stung you now have the pain of the slap and the frustration of failure. But the problem isn't what you think it is. So the practical joke has fooled you into practicing what is essentially an impractical idea. In some ways life, too, seems a practical joke, played on everyone in general by no one in particular. The only way to get free of the pain and frustration of our impractical practices is to replace our underlying false impressions with true ones.

That all our coping practices involve us in some interconnection reveals that we think the problem is being separate and in some way disconnected. We do not need to become astronauts or psychotics to dread disconnection. We do not need to be drowning or dying to fear annihilation. Most of our uneasiness can be traced to feeling separate, finite, and therefore unviable. The feeling that we could not survive apart gives rise to tremendous urgency to connect up to something. A mere snub, real or imagined, can bring us to this. And most of the connections we seek are in the form of others' attention. Recognition, admiration, obedience from others are the strands of our interpersonal, psychological connections. If we can get such attention from other people, we can ward off the feeling of separateness and the dread of not being at all.

Most parents want to reassure their babies that they are not alone. "I have to be there when he wakes up," they say, "otherwise he might think he is alone." That this is considered so necessary reflects the near-universal belief that to be alone is fearful and somehow life-threatening.[1] I remember what a revelation it was to me that my young child could be awake and alone in the dark quite happily. One night, after soothing songs and "Night nights," our baby settled down "enough so I could leave." I pretended to go out of the room, but instead I sat quietly in the dark. Seconds later I heard rustlings in the crib. Enough light filtered in through the window so I could see the little gowned figure haul himself up by the crib side. Rid of me, he was now free to go about his business. The bald/blond head glowed like a moon. Little feet made the mattress creak. Little wet breath came and went. "Uh? Uh?" piped the softly searching voice. "Uh? Uh?" Between each vocal sounding he waited, as one waits to hear the splash of a stone dropped into a well. But he called for no one. He was just sounding out the darkness. He did not seem to think he was alone. It was more as if he wanted to see how far he went.

But far beyond early childhood many people find solitude dreadful and abhorrent. It is not only drug addicts who seek a "connection." We all think the way to be sane and happy and safe is to stay "in touch," "connected," "integrated," "together." Connection is the method, self-preservation is the motive. By maintaining connections with others we seek to ward off or bury the fear of disconnection and annihilation.

A parent reported that he could tell when his son was unsure of himself by the volume of his music. The less adequate the boy felt, the louder the music. Every time there was an argument at home or a bad day at school, the stereo would be turned up. Perhaps the meaning of this common phenomenon is that faced with having to know how to live "on their own," teenagers are threatened in two ways: by being forced to confront the fact that they don't know how, and by being constantly told how by adults (which implies that they don't know enough). Not to know is life-threatening; being told only emphasizes the not-knowing. So the teenager "plugs in" to himself. "I hear, therefore I am." Loud music drowns out both the telling adult ("You don't know enough to live your own life, so you'd better listen to me") and the teenager's own secret inner voice ("I don't know how to deal with life on my own"). As the song says, it's a matter of "staying alive, staying aliiiiiive." *I am here. I exist. At least I am something to be reckoned with. I hear, I throb, therefore I am. If I can't hear you, I'm all right. If you can hear me, I must still be here.*

The "Look, Ma!" Position

Whenever we seem connected, we experience reassurance and, briefly, a sense of self-sufficiency or safety. But only briefly. Thrill of purchase, home run, pay hike, big deal, promotion, compliment—all such highs are orgasmic. They give us an intense experience of our selves as alive and viable, and then they are over. All are over in a moment. Now what?

Sometimes instead of seeking connections to others, we cope by seeking self-sufficiency and independence.[2] But even self-sufficiency is permeated by connection-seeking, as we try to pull together various parts of self: mind/body, action/emotions, head/heart, physical/spiritual. "I am trying to get in touch with myself," "to get in touch with my feelings," "to pull myself together," "to get my act together." Connection is sought when lack of self-sufficiency is experienced. Self-sufficiency is sought when connections let us down and we are thrown back on our own resources. But attempted self-sufficiency never lasts and is always fraudulent.

Earlier we spoke of a woman who recognized in her fear of her husband's death that she was depending on him for her identity as his wife. Her mother had been an incompetent, emotionally erratic alcoholic. Her successful father regarded his artistic son as a sissy, his wife and daughters as dumb dames. As a child, to become her father's preferred, best-loved child and make peace with the fact that she was female, she carved out for herself an identity as a better dumb broad than her mother. She avoided her father's disdain by playing dumb and never competing academically, by excelling instead in the "womanly arts." She became her father's best idea of a wife and devoted herself to wifehood and motherhood. Once she had recognized her tendency to depend on her husband and children for her identity as a wife and mother, she was freed from a lengthy spell of dreading her husband's death and grieving for her nearly grown children.

Soon thereafter it occurred to her that perhaps she was not as dumb as she had always seemed. By "dying" to her strictly "female" (loving, serving, receptive, dependent) definition of herself, the "male" (intelligent, assured, creative, independent) side of herself began to be born. Inspired to return to college, she was overjoyed to find that, indeed, her intelligence was not limited. She felt wonderful about herself—intelligent, free, and independent. Yet there was one strange thing. Although she was getting straight As, she was unreasonably nervous about speaking in class and often could not speak sensibly even when she thoroughly understood the subject matter.

One day, on an examination, she was asked to list in order the five relationships as defined in Confucianism. Number 1 was parent/child; number 2 was ruler/subject; number 4 was older sibling/younger sibling; number 5 was friend/friend. But she could not remember number 3. In the last few minutes of the exam she took a guess and wrote down "teacher/student." On the way home she was overcome with embarrassment as she realized it was "husband/wife" that she had left out, and that "teacher/student" did not belong on the list.

In counseling she recognized that although she had equated her newfound intelligence with self-sufficiency and independence, she was not yet free from her habit of relying on others for her identity. She had simply reattached her psychological umbilical cord from husband/parent to teacher/parent. She was embarrassed to think that the teacher might recognize in her wrong answer how childishly she looked up to the teacher and sought to be loved by her better than all the rest. She saw she had more spiritual growth ahead of her.

After her husband left her, another woman in counseling announced repeatedly, "I'm a much stronger person now—my own person. I have confidence in myself. I can stand on my own two feet." When I did not confirm this, pointing out that she was trying to replace her reliance on her husband by relying on me instead, she was very upset. "No, it's not true," she protested. "I am not dependent. I have always been very self-reliant. I had to be independent because I could never count on my husband for anything."

I said, "If you are so sure that this is so, then what is the tremendous need to get me to agree?"

"Oh, I see," she said at last.

Attempted self-sufficiency doesn't last. We run into our limitations. We know we aren't sufficient unto ourselves. We may fool others some of the time, but we never completely fool ourselves. Self-sufficiency is part sour grapes, part self-defense; and it is a lie. As the back-to-school mother's forgetfulness and the abandoned wife's pleas reveal, our self-sufficiency is suspect if we think we have to display it.

"Look, Ma! No hands!" is a declaration of both independence and of dependence. When a child can take her hands off the handlebars of her bike, she feels independent and free. She calls out, "Look, Ma!" because she depends on her mother to celebrate and affirm her newfound freedom. This is appropriate for a child. However, since parents often confuse the issue of celebration with approval and disapproval, praise and blame, most of us learn very early to do things *for* approval (and in fear of disapproval) rather than for their own sake. Long after we have left home we continue crying, "Look, Ma" to any candidate for parental support whose eye we can catch. When Ma looks at me, I am connected to her. "Look, Ma" says I depend on you to confirm that I do not depend on anything. Nobody is satisfied with secret self-sufficiency. Even as we pretend to be self-sufficient, we rely on others for recognition that this is true. From man in the street to president of the country, we are all in the "Look, Ma" position. In one wonderful cartoon a king confides to his jester, "All I want is wisdom, humility—and media coverage."

Religion as Reconnection

There is scarcely a time when we are not seeking interpersonal connections. If one connection fails, we latch on to something else. If a "good" connection is broken, outgrown, or outlived, we even grab for something bad. Given the predicament—connect or die—who can blame us?

A child of divorced parents spent equal time in his two households. Asked which parent he preferred to be with, he replied, "I just like to be wherever the electric train is." Wanting a stable connection, he had transferred his trust to a thing. Even alcoholics just want a "connection." They seek connection by reaching for a bottle. Alcoholics worship connection. So actually alcoholism could be called a religion, and the alcoholic a religious fanatic.

How can drinking be religious? The word *religion* comes from Latin roots meaning retie or bind together again. Alcoholics are at the end of their interpersonal ropes and want to re-ligate themselves or tie into something (to "tie one on"). So they reach for something to connect to—the bottle. Deprived or abused in childhood, as adults, when their interpersonal connections aren't holding up, finding life "on their own" untenable, they stoop to something else. Either way alcoholics are reaching outside of themselves, relying on something besides self and other to provide the feeling of being less alone and "falling apart"— and at the same time to numb the fear that comes with feeling disconnected, the fear of ceasing to be altogether, of altogether ceasing from being.

No alcoholic ever gave up drinking just because it was ruining his or her life or the lives of others. But Alcoholics Anonymous offers alcoholics a two-part way of discovering that there is no need either to hang on—to others or the bottle—or to be self-reliant. First alcoholics are introduced to the idea of a Higher Power, and then they are shown how to verify the presence of this Higher Power by relying on it "one step at a time." This is the only approach to alcoholism that works. It works because it is true. Whenever an individual is centered ("one step at a time") on truth (Higher Power), true, supportive power is revealed. This frees the individual from the need to grab onto anything lesser for support.

Everyone Is Religious

Actually everyone is an addict. We are people addicts. We don't want only love and companionship. We look to other people for more support than they are able or meant to give, not just for love but for life support of the self. As the drug addict abuses drugs by using them not just for physical medication but for psychological and emotional support, so we are inclined to turn to each other not simply for love and companionship but also for life support. An example is the man who cannot fall asleep if his wife goes to sleep first. There is a subconscious thought that unless his wife is aware of his existence it is dangerous for him to lose consciousness of himself. There is actually no physiological need for his wife to be awake in order for him to fall asleep, and yet he has a very strong experience that this is necessary. He regards her attention as being some sort of life support, her inattention as life-threatening.

So it is that the language of relationships is very similar to the language of addiction. In both contexts we use the words "support," "connection," "fix," "hooked," "use," and "abuse." From childhood on, psychologically unweaned, we remain people addicts. All recognized addictions are just substitution or consolation addictions to replace yearned-for people connections.

This idea deserves much further exploration, but here it is enough to point out that, to some degree, we all have this problem of wanting connections. We are all "hanging in there," held together by a thousand little threads. Like spiders dancing on their webs, we spend our days putting out, checking, mending, or reinforcing these threads. If others see you with this book, they may say, "Oh, are you religious?" But in this connecting sense everyone is re-ligious. We can only ask *what* is our religion? What are we seeking to tie into? Not whether, but whither.

When we think of religion as re-connection, it is clear that we have always been re-ligious, and not only on the Sabbath. From ancient times religion has reflected our desire to "come to grips" with life by getting reconnected to something "out there." But anyone interested in connecting could be called re-ligious. In a room full of people, if all interconnecting thoughts were replaced with pieces of string, there would be an impenetrable web. Interpersonal connecting thoughts are almost ceaseless: *Hey you, pay attention to me. See how sensitive, sexy, creative, helpless, strong, sweet I am. **Be** to me.* We can be re-ligious about money, recognition, relationships or, just to tide us over, even a bottle of booze.

Coping repertoires are re-ligious, connecting rituals. Certain routines in your repertoire are probably performed in ritual order. If one connection fails (your conversation with your mother is unpleasant or someone refuses to cooperate), you always turn to the same alternative (the TV guide); and if that fails (there is nothing on TV that turns you on), you invariably turn to the same further alternative (get in the car, chop wood, have a drink, take a bath, pick a fight). Instead of really living, spontaneously and joyfully, we seek to get through life safely—hand over hand, crossing through life as though fording a stream, by hanging onto one thing after another, never daring to jump into the stream of life and allow it to carry us along.

Whatever we turn to for connection becomes, at least momentarily, our idol, which we worship above all else for its life-sustaining potential. Praise, power, possession, and pulchritude are just some of the idols falsely worshiped for their ability to sustain the life of the self. But no matter how many connections we contrive to establish, they are never enough. They don't last. They backfire, break down, or turn sour.

One thing needs to be reemphasized. This discussion of our obsession with interpersonal connections is not meant to suggest that community, filial, friendly, marital, and parental relationships are not important or to be denied. The problem is our misuse of them for support other than they are meant to provide. The challenge is to find such a secure footing in life that we can be truly loving together; so that we can, in fact, truly love, rather than use and abuse each other.

Psychotherapy and Religion

When we feel completely let down by each other, psychotherapy and religion may become serious options. We tend not to turn to them until we have exhausted everything else. Psychotherapy requires an admission of personal inadequacy that some find threatening. Religion seems to require a leap of faith that feels risky, even ridiculous. So these attract us only when we are fairly desperate. Even if you were raised and have continued in a religious tradition, in a period of disillusionment or desperation, you may suddenly find yourself taking it much more seriously, overcome with either serious doubt or serious commitment.

The current proliferation of books, journals, conferences, programs, schools, and movements reveals how very many are exploring both psychotherapy and religion in the quest for peace of mind and wholeness—picking and choosing, mixing and matching. But what is the premise of the particular therapy, school, religion, or combination to which we turn? What do they say we are? To what do they propose to reconnect us? These are important questions, too often unasked.

Through religion and psychotherapy we seek to heal the disturbance arising from our sense of separation. But there is a re-ligious (connecting) and a spiritual (one-ing) approach to both. In both re-ligious religion and re-ligious psychotherapy we try to deal with separateness by *making* interpersonal connections, either human or divine. But in spiritual religion and psychotherapy, mental health and peace of mind are sought through discovering the presence of one fundamental source of life support and realizing our oneness (connectedness) with it. Although their methods may differ, spiritual religion and spiritual psychology are one whenever peace of mind or mental health are sought through the realization of our oneness with a fundamental reality (God or One Mind) beyond (though including) self and other. Nearly every great religion has a contemplative or mystical side founded on this conviction of essential oneness.

Re-ligious Psychotherapy

Strictly speaking, much psychotherapy is sought not as an alternative to the re-ligious or connecting way of life, but rather as an alternate re-ligion—that is, a way of making connections. At least this is what many people first seek from it. Viewing themselves as separate minds-in-bodies, called "persons," they want psychotherapy to help them form or re-form ties with other minds-in-bodies, to fix bad or broken interpersonal connections, reconstruct past ones, and establish new ones. Some also turn to psychotherapy for better internal connections ("to get in touch with myself"). They call this anticipated intrapersonal relationship with themselves "personal integration." Many aim at a balance between both interpersonal and intrapersonal relationships. Either way, interpersonal connections are being worshiped, and sometimes the relationship between therapist and patient is itself viewed as an important interconnection:

Another psychotherapist . . . who said a major reason for New Yorkers getting into therapy is that they are lonely and "not connecting" with other people said that [in summer when many therapists are away on vacation] the talk of absent therapists is so pervasive in New York that such commiseration has become an important way for people to "connect." . . . Patients deal with the separation [from therapists away on vacation] in a variety of ways, including the post-Freudian "Shopping Therapy" employed by one of Dr. K—'s patients, who pointed out that she has more money to spend when she does not have to pay for three

therapy visits a week. She supplements the shopping therapy with pe-
riods of hibernating, eating cookies and watching television.[3]

Repertoires! Connecting repertoires—if not to persons, then to
things, if not to things then self.

Re-ligious Religion

We may also approach religion in an interconnecting way, regarding God as the ultimate person to connect up to. Here the
mind-in-body person is trying to get reconnected to a God person. This God may be a mind-in-space rather than a mind-in-
body, but either way he is thought of as having (or being) a mind
not merely greater than but separate from our own. Adam got
kicked out of Eden, and ever since we have been trying to get
back into God's good graces, to reestablish the connection. Once
people probably just wanted God to give them food, land, rain,
victory. But once we see ourselves as minds-in-bodies or "persons," we also want a personal relationship with a God person.
Some say, "I have a close relationship with God." We wish we
had "a direct line to God," a person-to-person connection.[4]

Despite many differences between religion and psychotherapy, our ways of participating in both may not be so different. At
least initially we want them to help us negotiate connections
between persons, whether human with divine or human with
human. Whether interpersonal relationships are regarded as the
problem or as the answer, we tend to worship them. Whether
we are trying to get along with or without others, interpersonal
connections are the governing concern. When we think people
have betrayed us, we turn to God. When we think God has betrayed us, we turn to experts and friends. These days many disillusioned religious people are turning to psychotherapy, while
disillusioned psychotherapeutic people are turning back to God.
Both seek better connections.

The heart "longeth, yea panteth." Parched and yearning for
connection, we prostitute ourselves for strokes, pokes, pats,

kicks, and boosts of all sorts. Jesus spoke to the prostitute at the well. "Everyone who drinks from this water will thirst again, but whoever drinks of the water that I shall give them will never thirst. The water that I shall give them will become in them a spring of water welling up to eternal life."[5] What well? What water?

5. Seeing Through Life's Betrayals

Be ahead of all parting, as though it already were
behind you, like the winter that has just gone by.
For among these winters there is one so endlessly winter
that only by wintering through it will your heart survive.
RAINER MARIA RILKE

"On New Year's Day I had the day off, but—wouldn't you know, just my luck—my husband had to work," a woman complains. "So I got in the car and did a couple of favors for other people. First I went to my cousin's to deliver a gift. She took the gift but didn't invite me in because her house was a mess. Then I went to visit a friend who had said she was lonely. But when I got there, she said I couldn't come in because she was in bed with a man. Afterward I felt so resentful. I still do. I am always here for other people, but they just use me and are never here for me in return."

This individual is here for other people the same way that a fisherman is here for the fish. There is a hook in every gift she gives—a hidden attempt to appropriate the life of the other for herself. At one time or other we have all been fisherman and fish, and been disappointed and hurt in the bargain.

When life says no to us, it may not mean that we are never to receive the good we desire, only that our particular idea of good is in some way mistaken. For example, in the above story it was not the woman's unlovability nor her friends' unlovingness that was demonstrated in her failure to find the love she desired. It was her exploitative *idea* of love that proved itself false. Certainly we can all think of times when those we counted on for support betrayed our trust. Failing to provide the stable connection we seek, they have only exacerbated our sense of separation. Even psychotherapy. Even God. Maybe especially God? Are we meant to stand on our own then? Does this mean that we cannot count on each other? Or does it mean that we *need not* count on each other to the extent that we try to *because there is something else to count on?* If we count on that instead of on each other, will we then no longer care for each other? Or might we then at last be in love together?

What is it that makes relationships so disappointing and our desire for them so urgent? Remember when you slapped yourself because a mosquito was trying to bite you? It took only a couple of slaps before you turned around to discover that there was no pesky mosquito—only a pesky friend with a piece of grass. No more hurting yourself. No more worry about getting bitten. Simple. But when it comes to disappointing interpersonal connections, we are much slower to reach this turning point and the freedom it brings. We don't question the importance of connections or our idea of them or our right to them; we just work at them, stinging and feeling stung by whoever won't cooperate. However, if something is going badly, there are two possibilities: Either we are going about the right idea in the wrong way, or else it is simply a wrong idea in the first place—in which case there is no right way to go about it.

When I was a child, I came across something in the bathroom I had never seen before. It was some kind of tool—a cross between scissors and tongs. In fact it was my mother's eyelash curler. She told me it was a toenail clipper because she did not want me to blind myself. You cannot imagine how many hours I spent in the bathroom trying to cut my big toenail with her eyelash curler. It never worked. It never could work, because it wasn't a toenail clipper! This was trivial and harmless. But there are much more troublesome, time-consuming false ideas running much more of our lives. We cannot get free of them or their consequences until we recognize them as false and relinquish them in favor of something true.

There is no more troublesome idea than this: that we need to connect to each other *for some sort of life support.* For the most part, we don't even know there's an idea here. As far as we know, the only problem is luck, knack, cooperation. So the fact that we have just noticed our central preoccupation with this connection-seeking *idea* is quite important. The familiar Garden of Eden story sheds light on what we are trying to understand.

Adam's Apple: Where We Came Out

In Adam's story God is the betrayer.[1] On the one hand, God is Adam's creator and parent, his source of life, good, love, protection, approval—everything. God has created this little person and put him in a little heaven on earth where everything is perfectly wonderful. This is God the Parent, Person of Persons. Adam is dependent on God for everything. God is Adam's source of good.

On the other hand, it's a setup, a trap; and we just wait for Adam to blow it by biting into the forbidden fruit and getting kicked out—which he does. So God "cuts him off." Now he has to go out and struggle for his living—trying to be self-reliant, which he isn't, or to rely on something else, which he keeps finding he can't. It is not difficult to identify with this problem. So God is the betrayer—the source of expected good turned bad, unreliable. Adam would like to get back in good with God (reconnected), but God won't let him. Getting back into Eden turns out to be harder than crawling back into the womb. And, as a matter of fact, it is not a much different proposition.

Doesn't Adam's story remind you a bit of your childhood? Betrayal may be too negative, yet everyone who was ever a child has something in common with Adam. In the beginning there was someone we trusted for everything; with whom, visibly and then invisibly, we were umbilically connected; from whom came everything we needed. But in the end we had to go out on our own, relying on our own self or, that failing, on someone else. As life goes on, all selves, our own included, tend to prove unequal to the life support task we have assigned them.

This isn't very different from Adam's experience. Seeing the similarity, we already find solace. Although we may have felt uniquely inadequate or let down by others, we see that after all this is a universal predicament with which everyone has to deal. It is not a personal tragedy particularly inflicted on us by our particular parents—or, subsequently, with their stand-ins: spouse, friend, teacher, colleague, employer, child.

The Parentomorphic God, the Theomorphic Parent

Where did the idea that we need to get connected to others *for life support* come from in the first place? They say if a duck hatches next to a shoe, it just naturally assumes that the shoe is its mother. We assume our parents are God—particularly if they think so, too. And what parent doesn't? It looks that way.

Interconnection to persons appears to be at the heart of it all. From conception through sexual connection, from fetal development through umbilical and genetic connection, from infant nurture through nursing connection, from love through physical and emotional connection, and from child development through complex didactic and psychological connections, the child's being and well-being seem to depend on the parent connection. Parents, who are really channels of a life-giving, nourishing, guiding, loving life force, mistake themselves and are mistaken for the source itself. They are seen as primary creators, causes, and controllers of their children, which is to say that they are placed in the position of being God.

Ever since Freud we have tended to blame parents for their children's difficulties. This has a certain limited logic and benefit, but it also has certain problems. Parents are not God. They are not personally omniscient, omnipotent, or omnipresent. As often as they understand, they misunderstand; as often as they give, they must withhold; as accepting as they are, it is from parents that children experience the greatest threat of judgment and rejection. No matter how good family life is, it is inevitable that parent and child will part. Just as depending and growing up are built into the concept *child*, each one of these ideas includes its opposite.

Even parental success leads to betrayal. The more the parent

52 / COMING TO LIFE

succeeds in seeming to be *the* source of the child's good, the bigger the potential letdown when that source is withdrawn or outgrown—and the greater the desperation to replace it. So the most doted-on sibling may become a narcissistic adult, in just as much if not more psychological difficulty than the "rejected" sibling. Both have an insatiable desire to "make good" in the eyes of others in order to win further supportive personal attention.

No matter how smooth the transition from dependence to independence, it still leads to betrayal. The idea of becoming self-sufficient or grown-up is itself unrealistic and unreliable. Sooner or later we all encounter our limits. Then we want someone to take care of us, approve of us, agree with us, and keep us warm, supplied, and patted on the head. It is here that connecting/coping repertoires arise. It is in these repertoires that we meet the betrayer, which is anything we rely on for something it can't supply. So we keep meeting the betrayer—as provider/withholder, approver/disapprover, sustainer/let-downer, as parent, spouse, friend, sibling, employer, child, stock market, love connection, business connection, social connection, drug connection. Until we learn better this is the so-called "human condition": a fluctuation between the experienced unreliability of self and other. Not this. And not that other either.

The poignancy of this is expressed in the Adam story as a vicious circle. The child, who must grow up and become independent, begins to get ideas of its own, which the parentlike God says are no good, and for which God punishes the child by sending it forth to be on its inadequate own. Which is worse? Parents who think they are God? Or a God who acts like a parent? Same difference. Same dream. Adam himself is not presented as having parents, but clearly the originators of this story had parents after whom they modeled Adam's God.

Unmasking the Betrayer

Betrayal is associated with trust. When something trusted lets us down, we feel betrayed. But it may not be that somebody has truly betrayed us. More often we come to see that our trust was misplaced, our initial expectations false. Suppose a child climbing a tree steps on a weak branch. The branch breaks, and the child falls. Did the branch betray the child? Only secondarily. It was primarily the expectation that the branch should support him that failed.

The idea, not the branch, was proven false when the branch broke. Ignorance fell through! Ignorance always falls through. The branch is only weak in relation to the child's weight. It is not weak in relation to the weight of a sparrow. Then it is only ignorance that can be blamed when the child falls—not the branch, not even the child. Not self, and not other.

So perhaps it was never God that let Adam down—or Adam God or God us! Perhaps our parents did not fail us in the past, and we are not failing each other now! Maybe it has always only been some mistaken idea—a false expectation or ignorant assumption letting us down—a false *idea* of God letting down a false *idea* of self. Then we have met the betrayer, and he is false expectation. In re-ligious religion, it is a parentomorphic idea of God that lets us down; in re-ligious psychotherapy and interpersonal relationships, it is a theomorphic idea of parent that lets us down. But in every case it is an idea, a false expectation, that betrays us. It is never, at bottom, each other.

On the one hand, this is very upsetting. Is what we have been coping with our whole lives mistaken? Was our whole gritty bitterness and our true grit and the pearl of a person we built around it all nothing and for naught? Are we perhaps not martyrs and heroes? How disappointing! On the other hand, it is wonderful news. We have tried to change parents, spouses, children, and friends to suit our purposes, and that has failed. We have tried to change ourselves to suit our parents and spouses and children and friends. That, too, has failed. *I tried. I changed. I'm different now. What more do you want? I went to war and was a good soldier. Wasn't that what you wanted? Look, Ma, no **Arm!** Why won't you love me? Why won't you accept me? What more do you want?* But if the whole premise is false, if it is not how we are going about the problem but rather a fundamental misperception of what we are about—not evil but an error—then there is hope!

Connecting Is Itself a Betraying Idea

Ironically, the desire to survive underlies even the most self-destructive connecting behavior (whether to people, thing, or self). People commit or falsely confess to crimes that carry the death penalty in order to gain public confirmation that they are "really something." Soldiers are taught that if they die for their country, they will have really lived. When we say, "I am dying for a smoke," we express a strange idea that *smoking gives me the feeling that I'm alive.* A suicide note reads, "This is the only way I can feel I have power over my life."

Such contrariness is found even in seemingly wholesome self-preserving strivings for interpersonal connection. With frustrating consistency, they all work backwards. If we are especially concerned to appear intelligent (we seek our connection in the form of respect), we may become nervous, confused, thoughtless, inarticulate, and overbearing—effectively unintelligent! Music students complain that, although they can play well in private, they "fall apart" in lessons. It's easy to understand: When we are more interested in getting approval than in what we are doing, we don't do as well. If we desire to be loved, we may become coy, attention-seeking, manipulative, cloying, fawning, touchy—effectively unlovable. Children whose parents most desire positive (and fear negative) experiences for them become the most hypersensitive and easily hurt. Each self-preserving, connecting endeavor directly prevents what it is intended to achieve. Each produces the precise opposite of what is sought.

A young man, criticized and made to feel worthless in childhood, yearned to be loved. He strove to become so good, strong, intelligent, and thoughtful that others would see that he was wonderful after all, and so someone would want to marry him. But no one wanted to marry him. Because who could measure up to all that? Who wants to go around feeling less—less good, less talented, less thoughtful, less nice by comparison to her spouse? And he was making comparisons all the time, mentally building himself up by mentally tearing others down. Here he was working so hard to improve himself, to become superior instead of inferior, and his very success was almost more of a problem than his former shortcomings had been.

Even as we *choose* to engage in connecting rituals, this paradoxical dynamic shows up. In the very moment that, feeling threatened, we reach for a life connection to someone or something *other*, we abandon the actual life before us. In thought or deed, we deliberately depart the present opportunity to deal with past or future fears and fantasies. But here and now is all that ever really *is*—the only time to which the word *is* applies. So in turning away from the life before us, we are in essence choosing not to be. In dreading death and seeking to survive by making connections, we effectively cease from our being.

We observed that if something isn't working it could either be because we are going about it the wrong way or because the idea is mistaken to begin with. When it comes to connections, we have pretty well exhausted the first possibility. Is it not time to consider the possibility that connection-making may be a wrong idea that could never come out right? What is the idea again? There are two parts: first is that *to be disconnected means to die;* second is that therefore we need *to get connected to somebody or something*. Is there anything else to it? Yes. The underlying assumption is that *we are disconnected, separate, to begin with*. It is time to look at this assumption and the basis for it.

6. The Illusion of Growing Up

We all have secrets in our hearts. I will tell you one of mine. All my life I have longed to say yes, to give myself completely, to some Ultimate Someone or Something. I kept this secret for many years because it did not fit the image I wanted to present—that of an independent, self-sufficient man. The desire to surrender myself had been at least partially acceptable when I was a child, but as a man I tried to put away childish things. When I became a physician, and later a psychiatrist, it was still more difficult to admit—even to myself—that something in me was searching for an ultimate self-surrender.

Society, to say nothing of medical and psychiatric training, had taught me to say no rather than yes, to try to determine my own destiny rather than give myself, to seek mastery rather than surrender. For a long time, I tried to believe that I could learn enough and strengthen my will enough to take complete charge of my own life, but it never quite seemed to work.

I remember looking at some of my colleagues once, shortly after psychiatric training, and feeling deeply disturbed. They appeared to know what they were doing in life. They acted as if they knew what life was all about and how it should be lived, whereas I, in spite of all my education, was filled with more questions and uncertainties than ever.

At one point I even entertained the absurd thought that I had perhaps missed some specific chapter in some psychiatric text, the chapter that really explained things. My colleagues appeared to have read it, but somehow I had missed the assignment.

GERALD MAY

We know we are not self-sufficient. We cannot survive on our own. Even discounting our complex needs for love and laughter, we have to breathe and eat. We are not closed systems. Disconnected we could not live. Connection is vital. We know this. We have always known it. And we are not wrong. But what a time we have had trying to find an adequate, reliable interpersonal connection! We can't get along on our own; but connecting isn't working either. However, the basic idea that we are separate and disconnected, from each other and from everything else, is the one idea we have not yet examined. Where did it come from? What is its basis?

In the last chapter we looked at Adam's story as the story of how we got disconnected from God and thrown out of Eden. But now let's look at Adam and his betrayal experience for questionable assumptions. Now we approach the story in the light of existence. Our goal is to discover *what is* and *what isn't*, instead of what should or shouldn't be and whose fault it is. This can be considered a spiritual way of looking at things simply because ideas are not material; their substance is spirit. When we look at an experience or story for the *ideas* it expresses, we are beginning to look in a spiritual way. This is relevant to mental health or peace of mind, because now we are blaming mistaken *ideas* rather than people for our troubles. We cannot say that my mother's eyelash curler "failed" to cut my toenails. It was only the idea that it should cut toenails that failed. If you want to say it was my mother's fault, then you have to say that her idea of what was best failed. The fact that I got this idea from her doesn't matter. It was still an idea that failed.

Adam Reviewed

From a spiritual viewpoint we see some new things about Adam in Eden that did not meet the eye at first. In the beginning Adam is living comfortably and securely without question or doubt—literally taking things as they come, which indeed they are doing. *Hungry? Have some fruit. Lonely? Have some company. Idle? Have some work.* As need arises, it is all provided. Adam is neither grateful nor anxious. He is just living obliviously on the surface.

But then the serpent comes along and says, "Psst! Think of yourself!" The serpent signifies that what happened isn't Adam's or God's fault. It's just a low-level awareness—a ground-floor perspective. The serpent represents a viewpoint that is part of the process of becoming conscious. In the process Adam notices things. Well and good. The problem is that while he is noticing one thing, he is overlooking something else.

So the serpent says, "Pick it. Take it! Enjoy it! Why settle for less? Think of yourself." Your *self!* That's when Adam notices his self for the first time. Until then he's just enjoying the good of God as it comes. Now suddenly he's comparing himself to God and looking out for his *self!* This is when he starts *minding,* which is also when something begins to be the *matter.*

As you consider this, you may recall a time when you began to sense that there was something wrong with you that you would have to change in order to elicit, sustain, or regain your parents' love—a time when you began to live around approval and disapproval. It seems a matter of life and death. The parent is regarded as life-giver and sustainer. To keep getting this life we have to make sure that they keep loving us.

The concepts of parentlike God and Godlike parent arise from (or, actually, are handed down from generation to generation in) this moment of semiconsciousness we call self-consciousness. The moment we have separate selfhood, we have the whole experience of not being self-sufficient and of needing to be taken care of. This puts us in child/parent relationship to the whole universe. From now on we are always either trying to get taken care of or trying to get others to admire how well we take care of ourselves—which is just another way of getting others to take care of us.

At the age of forty one man was astonished to realize that he still looked at everyone as his parent—even the supermarket cashier. He didn't just want her to make change and pack his bags. Instead, he realized, he was doing everything he could to get her special attention, approval, affection, admiration, and encouragement. Even before his turn came he was hoping she would notice how handsome he was in his new shirt, how pretty his wife and child were. *My,* she should think, *hasn't he done well for himself?* His baby girl smiled. He glanced quickly to see if the cashier observed this. Would his precocious baby make all her precocious gurgles just as he stepped up to the register? "Like father, like daughter," she'd say—admiringly, dotingly. This seventeen-year-old ex-cheerleader—his *mother? Aren't you proud? See what I've accomplished? See what I've got? See what I've made of myself?* Or perhaps the reverse. He searched for pity in her eyes.

Poor guy. If he were my husband, I would certainly take better care of him. I would certainly make myself look more attractive than his wife does. He caught himself winking, gesturing, posturing, shrugging, and fawning at this seventeen-year-old *child!*—trying to get her to treat him the way his mother had or the way he wished she had—to be in any event for the moment his parent. He was appalled. How could he be so childish? He figured he must be nuts.

He isn't nuts or even extreme. What we have called our coping repertoire is really our collection of ways of dealing with not being grown up. We do this as if our life depended on it. If the bus driver won't make an exception and provide change, we feel rejected and unloved. It doesn't matter that he doesn't have and isn't allowed to make change. If he loved us, he would find a way. It isn't the change that's important; it's the love connection.

As long as we view ourselves as separate, we also regard ourselves as children. As long as we view ourselves as children, the whole world is our potential parent. Once this is clear, it also becomes evident that there is something off base about it. The childish idea that everyone should parent us—should in effect *be* for us—is clearly not quite right. So this must be another betrayer of an idea. Where does such a childish self-concept come from?

What really happened when Adam bit into that apple?[1] The serpent said, "When you eat of it, your *eyes* will be opened and you will be *like* God, knowing good and evil."[2] That's what happened. Adam's appropriation of the apple coincides with his seeing himself as *like* God, which implies that he thought he was *distinct from* God. With two eyes he saw double: Adam *and* God. It is really the story of the discovery of the separate self. Actually it is a pseudodiscovery, an invention, because it is mistaken. And that is the root of all the trouble.

Adam, the representative of immature humankind, comes to an immature understanding of himself by relying on an immature, insufficient mode of perception called the senses. This is what the serpent means by the opening of the eyes. Both of them. Two. Self and other. It is like seeing islands but not the earth that projects them, waves but not the sea of which they are a part. On the surface it seems so. Here I am in my skin. There you are in yours. Judging by what we actually see, feel, and hear, we seem disconnected from everything else—on our own, booted out into life. Helpless children. Betrayed, and somehow to blame. It is this misperception that gets us going. Whether as hotshots wanting admiration or waifs wanting adoption, we are all out to get connected.

Adam Splitting

Adam's apple is a beautiful symbol of the personal, skin-wrapped, mind-in-body self. It looks so whole and complete hanging there on the tree, like a thing all by itself. The stem is barely noticeable and seems unimportant. The shiny, red apple is so appealing. So he picks it. But at that moment it begins to die, because it wasn't separate; it was part of the tree. Of course the fall from the tree is not really the end of the apple, for even though its form will change, nothing of it will ever cease to be. Indeed, it is meant to fall as the fruitfulness of the tree. But that is another tale for another time.

The plucked apple symbolizes Adam's self-concept—the packaged deal—what you see is what you got—and it isn't enough and it is going to die. When Adam bit into the apple, which is to say that he swallowed the serpent's proposition, he effectively (perceptually) picked himself from God—his source of being, love, inspiration, vitality—very much as the apple loses its apple life in the picking. Or so he dreamed and, dreaming, went about his life, and so living began to experience. He wasn't such a sinner really—he was only "off his tree."

Adam Not-Yet-Two

Adam's is everyone's story—or part of it. It is not a story about obedience and picking fruit, but about consciousness. At first, like a babe who is safe and sound in his parents' garden, Adam is protected, watched over, and provided for, but unaware. He is just enjoying the surface of life, oblivious of its significance or the force behind it. When he needs a good idea, one occurs to him. He does not notice the occurrence; he just uses the idea. It is as if he were asleep, safe and sound, dreaming sweet dreams or none at all. We can call him Adam Not-Yet-Two. He is all of us in infancy.

Adam Two

Then, like a child beginning to be self-conscious, Adam notices himself. In particular it is *mind* that he encounters. He notices the importance of *ideas* behind things and events. Now when an idea occurs to him, he feels it in his head. He doesn't see it coming from outside, so he infers that it is his idea and he thought of it.

By claiming knowledge and taking credit for the thought, Adam also dreams up another possibility. Maybe he won't think of another idea. Maybe he will, but it won't be a good one. Maybe someone else has better ones, or more. The trouble is that now he's no longer listening. He's thinking that he's thinking—or ought to be or can't. As long as he is so busy with thinking, he is unable to receive whatever new ideas are coming his way from God. Jesus said, "Take no thought for your life . . ."[3] Adam represents the onset of "taking thought." He could not have followed Jesus' recommendation, because he has no idea of any intelligence beyond his own. As far as he knows, it is up to him to "mind" his own fort (except that somehow whether someone approves or disapproves of his ideas seems to be of momentous importance).

In third grade my piano teacher remarked that I played with "such beautiful, natural expression." I wasn't sure what she meant, except that if it was natural, I understood that it came from nature. For weeks after, hoping for further compliments, I played expressionlessly. I intentionally refrained from playing any dynamics at all, fearing that if I put expression into the music myself, it would interfere with what was coming from nature. It took a long time for my self-consciousness to subside enough to lose myself in the music again, allowing the music to express itself through me once more.

We didn't arrive at this thought-taking self-deception by ourselves. We had a lot of help. All through childhood we were being prepared, practicing manners so we'd know how to get on in the world, getting smart in school so we'd know "how to look out for ourselves." At the same time it was being suggested that if we did well adults would love and take care of us, but *that if we didn't, they wouldn't!*

So now the sleeping child has begun to dream the nightmare of separateness, which we call growing up. We can call him Adam Two. In child development this often really gets under way at about the child's second birthday and is called the "terrible twos." "Twos" is supposed to refer to the age of the child, but the experience really arises from the belief in two (or more) selves in conflict. Adam Two is still protected and cared for, but he believes otherwise. The belief feeds the experience; the experience feeds the belief. Ideas and opportunities are still coming, but Adam Two doesn't hear them because now he is fearful and distracted (literally "pulled from") his source by having his attention on something else. He thinks he is a body with a mind inside. With this achievement he has become mentally unhealthy—mentally un-one with the whole. He is "out of his mind," has "lost his mind" by losing contact with it. So our language is correct: we have "lost touch with reality." We aren't really disconnected, but we have lost sight of or not yet *seen* our oneness.

Adam Two is a pseudoseparate self going about the earth trying to get connected up again to something—he isn't sure what. He leans too heavily on things that are not meant to support him. They fail to meet his expectations, and he feels betrayed.

The Grown-Up Conspiracy

I am riding an elevator to the tenth floor. But the elevator stops to let someone off at six, and I get off, too, like a stupid sheep, just following and not looking out for myself. Letting myself be misguided by others makes me feel ungrown-up, sheepish. Why didn't I watch out for myself?

Our idea of grown-up is a mixed bag. Along with certain truly wonderful ideas of increased freedom and independence we have false ones about autonomy, self-sufficiency, and control. These can be summed up in a burdensome agenda of "mine is (or ought to be) the kingdom and the power and the glory." Relative to this goal we have a feeling of never being quite grown-up. The more we attempt to become self-sufficient, the more we see ourselves as separate. The more we see ourselves as separate, the more we are confronted with the fact that we are not self-sufficient.

On the one hand, we believe grown-up means being able to "go it alone." On the other hand, it is universally acknowledged that to be totally alone is not good. What we don't see is that the struggle to be self-sufficient is the avenue to separateness. When we are going toward self-sufficiency, we are going from God. We never really do get away from God, but our self-conscious thought-taking drowns out the guidance coming to us from Fundamental Mind, and prevents awareness of our oneness with God.

Job epitomizes the "achievement" of being grown-up. He did what Adam set out to do. He dedicated himself to becoming the best possible good and righteous grown-up child of God *in his own right*. Respected and admired, he is favorably compared to all others as the most righteous of men. He is God's best, most grown-up kid. But in distinguishing himself by comparison to others, he also established (in his dream) his apartness from God. Job's subsequent sickness and loss demonstrate that separate wholeness is no wholeness, separate goodness no goodness, separate life no life at all.

It is not so strange, really. Although all the noise and suction take place where the vacuum cleaner is, we know its real source of power is electricity. We are not surprised that the whole thing shuts down when the plug is pulled. But we don't seem to understand that in our very thought that we have to run our lives, we are unplugging ourselves from God. Only two things are ever happening: truth proving itself true, and the false proving itself false. Job is living *disproof* of the belief that "Mine is the kingdom and the power and the glory." It's a wonder we are so surprised.

In our minds "adult" means grown-up, which means not dependent on parents, self-sufficient. We mistakenly infer that to
be at once not dependent on parents and not self-sufficient
means to be doomed. Therefore, whenever we perceive ourselves to be not self-sufficient and no longer in a position to depend on parents, we feel driven to seek someone else to depend
on. So a conspiracy of connections is contrived. We seek outside
support to keep from "going under," while purporting to be self-
sufficient. In this guise of pseudo-self-sufficiency we hope to
have it both ways, maintaining secret connections in the form of
approbation for how self-sufficient we are. "Look, Ma, no
hands!" It is better summed up in the phrase, "My, my, aren't we
grown-up!" We would sell our soul, use any means at our disposal, to get this reaction from others. And why not? Our indoc-
trination began early.

In kindergarten, at the end of the morning, we were to go to
the cloakroom, don our outdoor clothes, and then wait in the
circle. One morning, while others still struggled with snowsuits
and boots, I happened to get mine on. Having nothing better to
do, I sat in the circle. "Just look how nicely Polly has gotten all
ready and is waiting in the circle," I heard my teacher say. How
sweet it was! I remember everything about the moment—what
kind of snowsuit I wore (blue, one-piece), how I sat (on my
knees), and where the voice came from (behind me, over my
right shoulder, somewhere near the cloakroom door). What else
could I do all by myself to get Miss Kennedy to love me for being
so grown-up?

A blind man realized that though he often needed assistance
in finding his way, he was inordinately resentful of anyone who
tried to guide him and was positively outraged if they did so
unnecessarily or awkwardly. Eventually he recognized that he
wanted to be helped in a way that made him appear sighted. He
was more interested in seeming sighted than in seeing the way.
Occasionally it occurred to him that he might actually be healed
of blindness. One day he was shocked to realize that whenever
this possibility came to mind, it was followed by serious doubt

as to whether it would really be advantageous to be able to see. In a subtle way, being a remarkably self-sufficient blind man had become what he now recognized to be his "thing," his means of getting admiration from others. What would he do "for a living" without it?

To any sighted individual, freedom to see is so priceless that it is unthinkable that anyone could question its value. So our immediate reaction to the confession of the man in the above story is that he clearly doesn't know what he is missing. When it comes to spiritual awakening, the Bible repeatedly suggests that we do not know what we are missing, either.

> Eye hath not seen, nor ear heard, neither have entered into the heart of man, the things which God hath prepared for them that love him.[4]

> Lo, this only have I found, that God hath made people upright; but they have sought out many inventions.[5]

> And this is the condemnation, that the light has come into the world, and people loved the darkness rather than the light.[6]

Spiritual awakening begins when the hope of "My, my, aren't we grown-up" dies. For most of us it is a long, reluctant dying to be born. A New Testament parable tells of a shepherd who gladly leaves his entire flock to rescue one lost sheep. In a way the lost sheep is the one who is most grown-up, self-sufficient. He knows himself apart from the flock. He is so grown-up that he has dared to go off on his own. Having thus established his separateness, he realizes he cannot survive apart on his own. Now he becomes the most rescuable sheep, the one most ready to appreciate being at one. He now recognizes the shepherd as savior, a guiding force beyond the flock. He is so happy to return to the flock. He welcomes companionship with the sheep, but he looks to the shepherd for guidance. He knows himself apart from his self. The rest of the sheep are still grazing in Eden's pasture. They are satisfied with grass; he is awake to grace.

Sooner or later it is inevitable for us to have Adam's nightmare.

It is precisely the nightmare that drives us to wake up. And when we wake, what will we find? For this we turn to a much later chapter in the story. By now Adam has matured, and so has the Garden of Eden. By now Adam has a new name: Christ. The Garden of Eden has a new name, too: the kingdom of heaven. There are others: Buddha, John, Moses, Meister Eckhart, and some among us. Each began where we begin, as separate selves in search of connections; but through spiritual awakening each arrived at a self-transcendent state of oneness and so became the only non-connection-seeking, the only unre-ligious people in the world.

"Self-consciousness" is actually semiconsciousness. Paul speaks of "life according to the flesh," which is not to do with sex so much as with the idea of being a self contained in a body. Eastern thought refers to the "illusory self." This misperception is the real problem because it leads to a mistaken idea of wholeness: the idea of the complete Me; me embodied; me *in corpus;* Me, Incorporated; Me, Inc.; Me, Limited (Ltd.). Henceforth we are in business for our selves. Seeing ourselves as separate, we aim to complete (become whole) our selves.

Sooner or later, hurt, frustrated, and exhausted by all attempts to achieve wholeness as completeness, we are forced to consider a radically different idea: wholeness as oneness. Like waves, leaves, sunbeams, and islands, everything—including our-selves—can be viewed two ways. Superficially they appear com-plete, separate things. But there is a deep, invisible oneness between each and its underlying source: island with earth, leaf with tree, light ray with sun. Each individual expresses the *uni*verse in *uni*que ways, and their relationship to each other is beautifully determined by the underlying reality from which each emanates. The same is true for us. Therefore our quest for wholeness takes place neither through self completion or inter-self connection, but through discovering what it is with which we are one and, then, being one with it.

7. Discovering a Spiritual Viewpoint

Willing to die,
you give up
your will. Keep still
until, moved
by what moves
all else, you move.
    WENDELL BERRY

Vast is That, Its form unthinkable, yet It shines smaller than the smallest. Far and farther than farness is It, yet It is very near, resting in the heart's heart.

                                            THE UPANISHADS

Jesus said, "I and the Father are one." He did not say, "I and my father have a good relationship." He did not say, "We are very close." He said, "I and the Father *are one*." This is a perception. He saw that God was his parent, which means that God was the source of his being. He saw that he and his source of being were substantially, in essence, one. Their being was one.

How amazing Jesus' statement of oneness is! It is non-re-ligious because it is nonconnecting. It annihilates the need to connect by annihilating separateness. It annihilates fear of being annihilated by the void by annihilating the void. It frees Jesus from the connecting quest. All our strugglesome clinging to each other is based on the impression that what lies between and beyond us is a void—a great gulping gulf that will sweep us away and swallow us up if we aren't hanging on to something. But what if Jesus' statement is true? What if it applies to us? If we could know that we are one with something beyond self and other, we wouldn't think we were apart. If we didn't think we were apart, we wouldn't have to go around all slung up between fear and betrayal, trying to get connected. If Jesus' statement applied to us *and if we could be aware of it*, then we, too, would be freed from the frustrating, interpersonal, connection-seeking quest that we have all been on ever since we first became self-conscious. If we and our life source are one, then we don't have to keep grabbing at each other for life support. If we can stop grabbing at each other, we won't have to keep pulling away, or climbing on top of, or struggling to get out from under each other. At last we can be together—freely, intelligently, and *lovingly*. So when we think of this statement, "I and the Father are one," we are in a position to be really interested.[1]

Don't Talk to Me about Your Jesus

Some people are distinctly disinterested in what Jesus has to say. They say, "Please don't give me any of that Jesus talk." When you even mention him, they think you are a religious fanatic, which makes them uncomfortable, which makes them mad. They want to slam doors, close books, and back off whenever they see you and your Jesus coming. The very name Jesus can be such a stumbling block that it seems wise to consider how we are calling on it here—and why.

What many react against is an interpersonal, cultic, connecting, re-ligious view of Jesus. In this view Jesus was God's special, only son whom God loved better than everyone else (and yet whom God sacrificed for love of the world). It gets very convoluted and hard to take. Jesus was so good and special that if you believe in him, he will save you, too—that is, if you are sorry enough for being as rotten as you are and lucky enough to get picked from among the rotten rest.

Some accept this idea and seek to buy into it. They say we are disconnected from God because of Adam with whom we are connected, but that we can get reconnected to God by connecting up to Jesus—like trying to get close to the president of the corporation by buddying up to his son. It's not what you are; it's who you know. The rest wander off still feeling disconnected, trying to band together (interconnection) or to be self-sufficient (intraconnection) because they don't buy it and can't do that. However, there is another view to consider.

Christian radicals say Christian fundamentalists are too literal, superstitious, and "hung up on Jesus." Fundamentalists accuse radicals of "doing away with the mystery" and "taking the Christ out of Christianity." M. Scott Peck points out that in essence *radical* and *fundamental* mean the same, and I have found this to be true. If I follow either the radical or the fundamentalist position as deep as I can go, I find that at root (*radix*) and at bottom (*fundus*) they come to the same awareness. Here, however, we begin at the radical side, which says that the personal, interconnecting, re-ligious perspective is not the only way of looking at Jesus.

Suppose, while lost in the wilderness, you come at last upon a sign that says "This way out." What do you do when you find this sign? First you rejoice; then, thankfully, you go where it points. Jesus was a living sign in the wilderness of ignorance, showing the way to reality. When connection-makers see the sign, instead of going where it points, they stop to worship it. As a result, nobody is getting anywhere. It is completely missing the point or, better, the pointing.

Jesus is more than a sign, he is also the road. Here we are at the crossroads, stuck, wondering which way to go, afraid to budge, but about to be run over. Or else we are trotting nervously a little way up this road, a little way up that one—afraid to go far in case it proves to be the wrong way. Now here comes Jesus dancing up and calling out joyfully, "It's OK! You don't have to guess and worry. I have followed this road and it is the one. Come on. Follow me. I will show you. I know. I've been there. *I am the way!*"

We could leave Jesus out of this discussion and avoid certain rutted notions and emotional potholes. We could veer east and take, say, the Taoist route, or completely abandon major highways and set off cross-country through the bush. Because believers are so definite about what they believe, and because nonbelievers are so definite about not believing that, such short-cuts seem attractive—except that they are not shortcuts.

For Westerners to travel by Eastern routes exclusively is like going to California from Illinois via Russia. If you want a trip around the world, you might do that. But you would call it a trip around the world, not a trip to California. To make our own way is like trying to go cross-country by traveling straight through a swamp rather than by the paved road around it. You might do that if you have a hovercraft and want to study the swamp. But then you would say you are going to study the swamp, not take a shortcut.

This is not to dismiss other traditions. Nothing has helped me to see my way along the Judeo-Christian path so much as Eastern lamplight.[2] Someone said that the various paths to enlightenment are like the roads to Philadelphia: the closer they get to Philadelphia, the closer they get to each other. But it's more efficient to begin where we are. We were brought up here, and we speak the language; we have played in the fields between these roads and crossed them time and again on our way to church and school and town. No need for other highways, only willingness to travel and a more up-to-date map. In this "country of our familiar," believers can get more out of what they believe in; the skeptical need not believe what they cannot. In our very own Judeo-Christian tradition and Bible, we have so much more to go on than we realize. And we have absorbed much more of it than we realize—if we can just see what it means, and what it has to do with everyday life. As a school-child I had to memorize chapter 12 of the book of Romans. God only knows what I thought it meant at the time, or what it meant to those who required this memorization. But now I am grateful for it. The phrase, "Be ye not conformed to this world, but be ye transformed by the renewing of your mind that ye may prove what is that good and acceptable and perfect will of God," is one of the ideas that rings my life.[3] To think I received it so long ago!

Seeing Beyond the Surface

Let's return to Jesus' fundamentally radical, radically fundamental statement, "I and the Father are one." How we live
depends primarily on how we see life. We know that much suffering stems from our struggle for connections, which stems
from a prior perception that we are separate. When Jesus says,
"I and the Father are one," he is already looking from a completely different perspective. Since he does not regard himself as
apart, he sees no need to make connections. Here are the two
big questions we have finally come to: With what reality beyond
his self does he see himself as being one? From what vantage
point does he get to see this?

There are two ways of looking at everything: a superficial way
based on sensory perception, and a deep way based on spiritual
perception. In the superficial way everything is regarded as a
separate thing in itself, just as it appears. This is how Adam
looked at himself, and how we tend to see ourselves. In the
deeper way everything is regarded as an indication of something
deeper or beyond itself. This is Jesus' perception—of himself and
of everything else. We also find such an idea in Buddhist teaching: "The one thing needful is to open one's eye to the significance of it all."[4]

We look at everything from one of these two points of view:
surface/sensory and deep/spiritual. On the decks of the *Nina,
Pinta,* and *Santa Maria* stood representatives of both. Seeing no
farther than the eye could see, the majority believed—*knew*—the
end was in sight. Only Columbus saw beyond what eyes could
see, and so sailed farther to break through the limitations of a
commonly held belief and set the whole world freer. We see some
things from the deeper perspective. By now we know what Columbus proved. When we look down a highway, even though it
appears that the road ends, we speed along, confident of its end-
lessness. We are able to look beyond the appearance.

When Albert Einstein was four, his father showed him a magnetic compass. This stunned the boy because it collided with his prior sensory perception that things could move only when acted on by "direct touch." He wrote:

I can still remember—or at least I believe I can remember that this experience made a deep and lasting impression on me. *Something deeply hidden had to be behind things.*[5]

This stood out in Einstein's memory because it was the first time he saw beyond the surface occurrence to its invisible oneness with a hidden force. He discovered the perspective Jesus must have meant when he said, "Judge not by the appearance, but judge righteous judgment."[6] "For we look not to the things that are seen, but to the things that are unseen," said Paul after him.[7]

Connecting Behavior

Sometimes we see beyond things; sometimes we don't. When we don't, we are likely to resort to rather desperate connecting behavior. This is when we get disappointed. For example, a child who thought the compass needle moved by itself and "knew" which way was north might break the compass in order to acquire (connect up to) the powerful needle. How disappointing it would be when the needle just lay there!

I remember a similar disappointment from my childhood. The best thing about my doll was her eyes, which I thought beautiful and lifelike. Eventually Gracie deteriorated—aided and bedwetted by my baby brother, who had also taken a shine to her. To my chagrin, during each nap he soaked up her charms, but she just got soaked. Finally my parents said Gracie had to go, melting my initial resistance with promises of reincarnation—a brand new (odorless!) Gracie! That's when I decided to "save" her eyes. It was a moment both dreadful and wonderful as, alone in my bedroom, I prepared to smash her bedraggled head and extract the two still-beautiful blinking eyes. But excitement quickly turned to horror as soon as the doll's eyes rested in my hands. Out of her head, Gracie's eyes were dead—not beautiful, not lively, just two odd inanimate things connected by a metal band. I threw them away.

All through life such destructive behavior and betrayed expectations are natural by-products of reliance on a superficial perspective. The superficial perspective leads to stupefaction, misunderstanding, and often to destructive, connecting behavior. Deep-seeing, on the other hand, leads to increased understanding, freedom, and rapport or oneness with life.

Seeing Beyond Self and Other

When we see beyond appearance, it is usually because someone showed us. Certain insights are common knowledge. "Ha ha," we laugh, "how dumb to think the world is flat!" But everybody saw it that way. Everyone *knew* it was flat. Except Columbus. He saw beyond without someone explaining it to him! So a good question is, From what perspective did he see beyond where others had seen before? The answer is, from the deep-seeing perspective. Some idea of *what must be so* overrode his sensory impression of what seemed to be. This ability to see beyond appearances allowed him to take the risk that led to a realization that burst the bonds of human ignorance and catapulted the whole human race into a much larger realm of freedom.

Throughout history and in every field of discipline there have been those who made breakthroughs. Whatever the breakthrough, it came from looking at the deeper significance of a surface appearance—first perspective, then understanding. Columbus looked beyond the geographical horizon. Jesus shows what happens when we look beyond the horizon of self.

We see through many things, but there is one place where we do not see through at all. We still see people, especially remarkable people, in the superficial way, as having or containing powers and virtues. Jesus had *special powers*. Einstein had *a better brain*. As I took out my doll's best part for keeping, when Einstein died, his brain was removed for scientific study.

On December 31, 1978, a small notice tucked away on p. 17 of the first section of the *New York Times* announced that at the time of his death in 1955, Albert Einstein's brain had been removed from his body and entrusted for study to a team of experts headed by Dr. Thomas S. Harvey, the pathologist at Princeton Hospital where Einstein died. At the time Harvey had said that although "it looks like anybody else's [brain]," clues to the source of Einstein's genius would be sought in the tissues and fluids that remained.

Now twenty-three years later on the eve of the celebration of the centennial of Einstein's birth, Dr. Harvey has still not announced any results. The *Times* reporter speculated that this was perhaps due to the fact that even after careful study, Einstein's brain still looked like anyone else's.

When all is said and done, then, is it just an ordinary brain? "No," Dr. Harvey says. He had met Einstein, spoken with him just before the great man's death. "No," he says again. "One thing we know is that it was not an ordinary brain."[8]

Surely there is value in such research, and in 1985 a physical difference was found in Einstein's brain that explained his superior ability to see connections. However, it was noted that the brains of rats free to play in unusually large, well-equipped cages also developed this difference. Was it nature, or nurture, or something more? Whatever the answer to this popular debate, we can see how helpful it is to look at each appearance as the manifestation of hidden forces or conditions beyond itself. Sensory perception alone simply does not give us enough to go on. At least we can say that there is more to be seen, and more to be gained.

Therefore, as we seek breakthroughs in our own quality of life, it is helpful to consider in the deeper way these two outstanding individuals, Jesus and Einstein. I do not mean to equate them or their contributions. My reason for bringing Einstein into this discussion is to elucidate a fresh, helpful way of looking at Jesus, and to show that the issues are really cognitive and spiritual rather than personal or religious. Both men were really scientists. Einstein was a natural scientist, Jesus was a scientist of being. Our goal is to discover how these great seers saw what they saw. Einstein started with the universe and was working his way toward being. Jesus started with being and was working his way toward the universe. Inevitably they meet in the same place: God.

To understand Jesus' declaration of oneness with God, we have to look at him as he looked at everything: in the deep-seeing way, for significance. We are used to looking at waves that way. We do not regard them as separate water-selves hurling themselves into little peaks and marching around willfully on the face of the ocean. We know they manifest the nature and action of the sea beneath, that waves and sea *are one*. Our goal is to learn this way of seeing everything, especially people, eventually ourselves.

We are used to looking at words, deeds, and facial expressions as significant of people's hidden thoughts and feelings, but we are not used to looking at people as significant of anything beyond themselves. This is what we must learn in order to benefit from Jesus' statement, "I and the Father are one." It is what he had to do in order to make his discovery. Because that's what it is. It isn't a personal claim, but a firsthand scientific discovery about selfhood in general. Eureka! My *am* and God's *is* are one! My self and my life source are one. In his own way Albert Einstein began to understand this, too:

A human being is part of the whole, called by us "universe," a part limited in time and space. He experiences himself, his thoughts and feelings as something separated from the rest—a kind of optical delusion of his consciousness. This delusion is a kind of prison for us, restricting us to our personal desires and to affection for a few persons nearest us. Our task must be to free ourselves from this prison . . .[9]

Human Compasses

People can be viewed in the same two ways that we have viewed the compass, with the same divergent results. The deeper way leads to increased understanding, freedom, and love. The surface way, in which brilliance and goodness are regarded as self-contained personal powers, leads at best to unconstructive personality cults—and at worst to destructive connecting behavior. So the child might smash the compass to get the needle. So Columbus's crew plotted to take his life in order to hang onto their own.

As seemingly separate selves we want to connect to whatever will contribute to our self-sufficiency or compensate for our lack of it. If the child sees the compass needle as smarter than he is, he says, "I want that." Smash! When Adam compares himself to God, he wants what God has! Pluck. From the superficial perspective we can only make comparisons between self and other. Whatever others seem to have that we can't get, we want to destroy. If they can't have what Jesus has, some don't want him to have it either. So the desire to destroy his credibility or even Jesus himself arises.

All our really awful greedy, grabby, grappling ways of being with each other spring from the superficial perspective of self and other. This explains how, in the name of love, we wind up being so *un*loving. So an unsure man yearning to return to his mother's care becomes overly preoccupied with his wife's breasts. Wanting love he tries to acquire what he imagined to be the source of his mother's power, even to take revenge against her for withholding or ruling him. His wife, feeling like "nothing but a sex object," backs off. The more she backs off, the more forcefully he pursues her breasts, not only fondling, but hurting them. The only possibility of ever freeing ourselves from these destructive ways and finally truly being in love together depends on the deeper viewpoint.

On the surface the compass is exceptional because, though inanimate, it "moves" and, though brainless, "finds" the north pole. On the surface Einstein seems exceptionally brilliant. On the surface Jesus seems the most exceptional of all. Some wonder if he truly walked on water, changed water into wine, healed the sick, raised the dead, came back from death, and appeared as pure light with others supposedly long dead. Even those who are not sure what to make of such accounts can benefit from a deep look at the remarkable figure at their center.

Even if we do not yet know what to make of the "miracles," Jesus is also known to have *been* in ways that we find very desirable. By all accounts he was exceptionally loving, unencumbered, forgiving, peaceful, free, and unafraid. He did not doubt his purpose in life. He was sure, even in the face of death, of the fundamental goodness of God. He was sure there was life beyond the horizon of space and time. So, however we regard the miracles, we—who have everything but are happy with nothing, who are bitter against the past, in some way afraid of death every moment of life, and to a large extent in hate with each other—can't help but yearn to understand this remarkable individual.

Because we regard the compass as *significant* of something beyond itself, we are able both to read and to reproduce it. The result is that now the whole world does not have to stay home for fear of getting lost, and is not dependent upon only one compass for navigation about the globe!

Jesus urges us to look at him in this same significance-seeing way, not as an exception. Even when he refers to himself, it is as a manifestation of something beyond himself. "Think not that I am come to destroy the law or the prophets; I am not come to destroy, but to fulfill," he says.[10] "Why callest thou me good? There is none good but one, that is God . . ."[11] "The son can do nothing of himself but what he seeth the Father do . . ."[12] "My Father worketh hitherto and I work . . ."[13] "He that hath seen me hath seen the Father."[14] He repeatedly suggests that there is something deeply hidden beyond the self that we do not yet see. If we saw it we would no longer be dependent on him for our celestial navigation. Jeremiah predicted such a time: "And they shall no more everyone teach their neighbors, saying, 'Know the Lord,' for they shall all know me from the least of them to the greatest of them."[15]

By looking at the compass in the deep-seeing way, we discovered a hidden, physical force on which we can rely wherever we go. By looking at Jesus in the deep-seeing way, we discover certain forces and laws of being on which we can rely as well. Through conscious oneness with these laws, we too can manifest some of the qualities we have so marveled at in him. Jesus said as much. "Truly, truly I say to you, whoever believes in me will also do the works that I do," he says, "and greater works shall you do because I go to the Father."[16]

It is clear. It makes sense. We who have seen the compass have recognized magnetism at work. What is at work in Jesus' life? Already better questions are coming, the same ones that allowed us to duplicate the compass. In what way is Jesus one? With what deeply hidden reality? Under what conditions was this so wonderfully manifest?

If we were Buddhists, we would say "Not two" and leave it at that, since it is belief in more than one power that is the basis for all depravity and suffering. But in Jesus we have a more explicit guide who proved that life is not a matter of surface connecting, but of deep seeing. He answers all our connection-seeking questions by pointing to spiritual perceptivity, the avenue of conscious oneness. Our questions are all connection-oriented and concerned with getting and having. His answers are all oneness-oriented and concerned with seeing.

We say: I am hungry. I lack. I want.

He says: I have meat to eat that ye know not of. My meat is to do the will of him that sent me.[17]

We say: I'm thirsty again. Nothing quenches.

He says: Whoever drinks of the water that I shall give them will never thirst: the water that I shall give will become in them a spring of water welling up to eternal life.[18]

We say: I want fulfillment. I want to be good at something, creative.

He says: There is none good but one that is God the Father.[19] The Father worketh hitherto and I work.[20] The son can do only what he *seeth* the Father do.[21]

We say: I can't find peace and happiness anywhere. I haven't found my niche.

He says: The kingdom of God is within you.[22]

We say: But there is so much evil and darkness. I feel we are powerless to overcome it.

He says: Judge not by the appearance; judge righteous judgment.[23]

We say: I don't know what to do; I feel trapped and at a loss.

He says: Know ye the truth and the truth shall make you free.[24]

8. Guided by Living Compasses

The man pulling radishes
pointed the way
with a radish.

ISSA

Listening with the single ear and seeing with the single eye . . . the seeing being seeks oneness with the One Mind as conscious awareness of what is . . . To the Seeing Being everything is a word. Like words themselves the seeing being regards everything he sees as a symbol, as points where ideas become manifest. The seeing being is himself a word of God—the turning point between divine idea and divine expression, between divine cause and divine effect, between intelligence and love. Becoming as a child, the seeing being understands that the whole point of seeing is not doing or having but being. And so it is that the true seeing being with all his understanding is not after all preeminently knowledgeable but preeminently loving.[1]

We are lost; we do not know the way. We have difficult choices to make. We seem stuck with such wrong ones! Which way should we go? We could almost envy the compass. Not only does it show the way, it is itself so guided and sure. Not only do Jesus and Einstein point the way in religion and science, they are so guided and sure in life. How? By what? When we examine their lives for the answers to these questions, we find not merely ethics or physics, but the true nature and way of life.

What have these great people to do with us? They seem so far above, so out of reach. Yet they were not so exceptional. Einstein had painful, unyielding family problems. He must have known what it is to suffer and question. Alone in the wilderness, alone in Gesthemane, alone on the cross, even Jesus was tempted.

They were on a higher plane, maybe, but not from another planet. Unique individuals certainly, but not extraterrestrials.

So now we will look beyond them as we looked beyond the compass—not only for the directions they give, but also for what lies behind and moves them so consistently in the right direction. The compass is not and does not understand the gravitational force, yet is an expression of it. Einstein and Jesus are not the force—of God, of higher intelligence beyond them—and do not claim to comprehend it. Nevertheless they manifest it as "living compasses" by which we all can find our way. What is this force? How does it become so beautifully manifest in an individual life? How does a "living compass" work? The important questions we are working toward are these: Is there something out there that I can trust with my life? Is there a Higher Power than persons? And, if so, how can I know it and let it take over?

Being of One Substance

To work, the compass must meet two conditions of oneness— of *substance* and of *stance*. The first is a condition of substantial oneness. The compass, though separate, has one quality in common with a force beyond itself: magnetism. Unless the needle is magnetic, it cannot work. Wooden or plastic replicas are useless. It is in this one invisible quality of magnetism that it is one with the deeply hidden magnetic force running through the earth's core.

To function as an intelligent, loving "living compass," the individual must mentally meet the conditions of substance and stance that the compass fulfills physically. As in magnetism the compass is one with something beyond itself, so it is in awareness that we are one with something beyond ourselves, in particular with Fundamental Mind. To differing degrees Einstein and Jesus both knew this. They both recognized that the substantial factor in their lives lay not in flesh, bone, or brain, but in perspective. Said Einstein: "The essential in a man of my type lies in what he thinks and how he thinks, not in what he does or suffers."[2]

Therefore Einstein's autobiography records not events but unfolding awareness. To him the most important issues were perceptual. He was a scientist. To him life was awareness. He was not interested in making connections but in seeing connectedness. Whereas others seek discoveries in order to connect to admiration, power, wealth, Einstein sought to see for the sake of seeing. Others work for a living. Einstein lived and worked to see.

Jesus proclaimed his oneness with something beyond the self in his "I and the Father are one" declaration. As to the nature of this oneness, he said, "The eye is the lamp of the body."[3] The eye is for seeing. Through seeing we are one with the light; through perspective with truth. To see means to be aware. For Jesus, too, awareness is the essence of the individual, the substance of his oneness with a force beyond the self. "The son can do only what he seeth the father do."[4] He saw us all as primarily seeing beings.

Seeing from One Standpoint

The second condition of oneness is stance. Standing on one foot the compass needle *relies on* a deeply hidden force more than on surface factors. It must also be *free from* connection to anything else. If it is attracted, attached, or bumps into anything on the surface, the action of the underlying force is obscured. The force still acts on it; but instead of being drawn into northward alignment, it gets stuck, bound by friction, seemingly paralyzed instead of seemingly animated, seemingly stupid instead of seemingly intelligent.

For us, as seeing beings, the equivalent of stance is standpoint, and we find both Jesus and Einstein conducting their lives and work from a one-pointed perspective. Each was motivated by a profound conviction that there is fundamental unity to reality. To discover this oneness was their number one priority and ultimate concern. They counted on it. The idea of oneness drew their attention, kindled their passion, and ran their lives, just as magnetism physically attracts and governs the compass.

The Conviction of Oneness and the Question of Evil

Einstein knew in his heart that there had to be a fundamental oneness to reality:

It is a wonderful feeling to recognize the unifying features of a complex of phenomena which present themselves as quite unconnected to the direct experience of the senses.[5]

If we were not aware of the oneness, it could only be that we had not seen it, not that it didn't exist. We would simply have to go deeper. His conviction was so deep as to be theological.

Quantum mechanics is very impressive. But an inner voice tells me that it is not yet the real thing. The theory produces a good deal but hardly brings us closer to the secret of the Old One. I am at all events convinced that HE does not play dice.[6]

In the fall of 1919, in the course of a discussion with a student, Einstein handed her a cable which had informed him that the bending of light by the sun was in agreement with his general relativistic prediction. The student asked what he would have said if there had been no confirmation. Einstein replied, "Then I would have to pity the dear Lord."[7]

Nature hides her secret because of her essential loftiness, but not by means of ruse.[8]

Jesus, to express his conviction of oneness, expanded the great Shema, the fundamental Hebrew teaching on which he was raised:

Hear O Israel, the Lord our God, the Lord is One. Thou shalt love the Lord thy God with all thy heart, and with all thy soul, and with all thy mind, and with all thy strength. This is the first and great commandment . . .[9]

Here he also emphasizes the importance of oneness as a first priority. "If thine eye be single," he said, "thy whole body will be full of light."[10] Otherwise, at least in the Bible proper, he did not explicitly speak of oneness, except his own oneness with God. What alternative evidence is there that he was so convinced?

Neither Einstein nor Jesus could reconcile himself to inconsistencies. To them conflicting "truths" were unacceptable in relation to their deep-seeing conviction of oneness. Einstein was concerned with the nature of physical reality, Jesus with being. This involved Jesus with the question of good and evil. As Einstein could not accept two conflicting truths about physical reality, so Jesus could not accept two conflicting natures to being! To Jesus the idea that *God is all loving and all powerful*, and the inference from human suffering that *God is either not all loving or not all powerful*, could not both be true!

Jesus' followers turn to him for help with the harsh realities of suffering. A meeting of two conflicting ideas—life and death, abundance and lack, health and sickness, love and hate—can be called a *harsh reality*. But Jesus and (with respect to physics) Einstein share an unshakable conviction that harsh realities cannot be fundamentally true.

Any idea of fundamental oneness includes efficiency, order, harmony, reasonableness—all of which can be summed up and would be manifest as goodness or love. Discord, disharmony, inconsistency all depend upon conflicting factors. There could not be discord without opposites. The existence of chaos or evil would depend on there being one thing in opposition to another. So at some level evil and good could not both be fundamentally true. Evil experience, though undeniable, must not be as solid or immutable as it seemed. Somehow there must be a way to see through it! Through physics Einstein also approached such an astonishing conclusion. "Subtle is the Lord," he said, "but malicious he is not."

We spend so much of our lives fighting to ward off or overcome certain evils. But the conviction of oneness is actually a conviction of life's essential goodness. Perhaps this is why Jesus said, "I have yet many things to say to you, but ye cannot bear them now."[11] Perhaps it was too big to say or too hard to hear; perhaps it was not something to tell but to show. Perhaps he knew we had to see it for ourselves. Could it be that he had not finished seeing it for himself?

However little Jesus said, his existential statements (ideas expressed by the way he lived) evince his conviction of life's essential oneness *and goodness*. We find him constantly "taking evil on," challenging it by inviting the blind to see, the paralyzed to walk, the insane to be sane, the wicked to be good, the dead to awaken, finally even staking his own life on the conviction that death would not be the end of him. His whole ministry expresses the pervasive conviction that life, not life *and* death—health, not health *and* sickness—good, not good *and* evil—and love, not love *and* wrath, were fundamentally so.

The implications are offensive because they drastically collide with our experience of suffering and evil. Suddenly we are almost against what we are for. We came for help with sickness, death, evil, but we are not so eager to hear that they are not all that they seem to be. Sympathy, yes. Help, yes. Praise, yes. Encouragement, yes. But healing? transcendence? awakening? On the other hand, what if we really could be freer—become healed, whole, peaceful, in love?

It is not only for ourselves but also out of compassion for others who suffer that these ideas have to be looked into. At the very least they bring hope and give direction that is truly practical and helpful. It is important to start small, at home—with our mere apathy, grief, lack of confidence, tension headaches, strained relationships. When we are apathetic or depressed, we are dead to life. When we feel lack and envy, we share the same greedy mentality that leads to Third World starvation. When we squabble with each other, we contribute to global power struggle and war. Global problems are collective versions of individual confusions.

So if we can be healed of *any* of these, we will have helped to bring the dead to life and to make peace and love. But we have to start small and now and here.

Detachment

If there is something to the idea of oneness that can benefit us, the question is, *how can we get to see it?* How did Jesus become aware of it? This brings us back to the vantage point from which he regarded everything, his standpoint. We know he relied absolutely on a conviction of oneness. We also know he did not rely on anything else for his security. All usual, supportive connections to home, family, career, recognition, Jesus denied himself. "Foxes have holes and birds of the air have nests, but the Son of Man hath no place to lay his head."[12] He sought to free himself of reliance on everything other than God. Already as a child he said to his own parents, "Why seekest thou me? Wist ye not that I must be about my Father's business?"[13] And subsequently, in the wilderness, fasting from food and isolated from all contact with people for forty days, it is written that the devil tempted him. He was tempted to rely on food and fame and personal favoritism. He craved what we in our self-doubt have craved.

Then Jesus said to him, "Get thee behind me Satan! For it is written, Thou shalt worship the Lord thy God, and him only shalt thou serve."[14]

Jesus' abstinence was neither self-denial nor self-reliance. It was the cognitive process through which he was able to discover a reliable force beyond self and other. Gautama, too, alone and fasting beneath the Bo tree, suffered such cravings and resisted such temptations before his absolute reliance on the transcendent led to realization of his oneness with the Buddha.

But the Buddha rose like a lotus from stagnant water whose petals are unsullied by muddy drops, and saw the world clearly, with a Buddha's serene eyes.[15]

Einstein? Jesus? Buddha? What is the point of dwelling on such outstanding individuals? The point is not to let them go to waste. The point is to see what they have to do with us. We do not have to sail off the end of the earth to prove that the world is round, because Columbus did it. But we do not get the benefit of his breakthrough—the greater freedom he won for us—if we only stay at home. We do not have to fast for forty days in the wilderness or die on a cross to prove that we will not die if no one is thinking about us. We do not have to do this, because Jesus did it. But we do not get the benefit of his breakthrough unless, within the framework of our own immediate lives on our own immediate frontiers, we test out for ourselves what he proved, letting go of what he let go of in order to prove to ourselves what he proved and to go where he went.

It is the same as the way the compass works: not only standing on one foot in the deeply hidden, but also remaining detached *from* everything else. The mental equivalent is devoted attention, commitment, interest, or worship. As the compass needle rests only on one slender point and not on anything else, Einstein staked his career and Jesus his life on this idea of oneness. While we waste our lives trying to prove ourselves to others, both men took huge personal risks. Einstein's single-minded devotion to uncovering the deeply hidden oneness freed him from many distracting worldly attachments to pursue less popular and profitable lines of research. Even as a young scientist, when a respectable academic post did not come easily, he readily accepted the lowlier job of patent officer where (however much in obscurity) the undemanding work left him freer to pursue his primary interest, the unified theory of relativity. So the idea of oneness drew and drove him. "Following his bliss," yielding to the pull of the deeply hidden on him, he allowed it to make him a living compass pointing the way for all physicists.[16]

As in all great spiritual scriptures, recommendations of detachment abound in the biblical record of Jesus' teachings. He knew that for the deep-seeing oneness to be realized, the superficial, interconnecting perspective had to be relinquished. Nothing else could be clung to or counted on for life support—neither persons, nor possessions, nor prestige, nor profit.[17] This is what Buddha taught as well:

> Craving is like a creeper,
> it strangles the fool.
> He bounds like a monkey, from one birth to another,
> looking for fruit.
>
> When craving, like a poison,
> takes hold of a man,
> his sorrows increase
> like wild grass.
>
> When this terrible craving,
> fierce to subdue, is subdued,
> Sorrow slips off like
> drops on a lotus leaf.[18]

Not Self-Sacrifice

Like Columbus and Buddha, who left family and security to sail beyond the horizon, Jesus appeared self-sacrificing. But the verbs he chose for his exhortations and parables about detachment (to seek, be about, savor, take thought, worship, serve, love, hold to, follow, be with, care for, take seriously) show that his concern was to free attention from preoccupation with one thing in order to achieve awareness of another.

In the parable of the seeds he says, "He also that receiveth the seed among thorns is he that heareth the word: and the care of this world, and the deceitfulness of riches, and the lusts of other things entering, choke the word, and it becometh unfruitful."[19] The family, things, ambitions, pleasures we rely on are thorns that snag and hold our attention. Jesus saw nothing intrinsically wrong with them, only with our mental attachment to and reliance on them. He knew that to exist in loving, healthy, harmonious relation to these aspects of life without first establishing our oneness with the underlying force that harmonizes them is not possible, any more than we can walk without reference to the law of gravity.

Two otherwise cryptic passages also make sense in this light: "No man can serve two masters, for either he will hate the one and love the other: or else he will hold to the one and despise the other. Ye cannot serve both God and mammon."[20] "Whoever gathereth not with me scattereth abroad."[21] We cannot have two *uppermost* concerns, for either we will be disinterested in one and interested in the other; or else we will be aware of one and ignore the other. We cannot pay attention to two things at once. Anyone who is not focused on oneness is distracted by everything.

Jesus did not mean for us to give up family, things, success as such; only to free our consciousness from secondary surface concerns in order to become aware of something deeper and more reliable. First things first. Only by fulfilling the first commandment to love God above all would it be possible to (and impossible not to) fulfill the second (which is "like unto it") to love each other.[22] Only oneness with the whole leads to oneness with each other.

In comments about a fellow physicist, Einstein spoke along similar lines. He pointed out that the seemingly selfless devotion of his colleague to more difficult, less profitable scientific research was not due to virtuous self-sacrifice:

The longing to behold . . . preestablished harmony is the source of the inexhaustible persistence and patience with which we see Planck devoting himself to the most general problems of our science without letting himself be deflected by goals which are more profitable and easier to achieve. I have often heard that colleagues would like to attribute this attitude to exceptional will power and discipline. I believe entirely wrongly so. The emotional state which enables such achievements is similar to that of a religious person or the person in love: the daily pursuit does not originate from a design or program but from a direct need.[23]

To what need is he referring? The need to *see through*, and thereby discover the underlying oneness beneath diverse phenomena.

By Their Fruit

The compass can be trusted, because it is not erratic. We trust its directions, because we see its own directedness. The same is true with Jesus and Einstein. We can trust the direction they give, because their unusually creative and beneficial lives are living proof of its validity. Existentially they speak as ones "having authority."[24]

Einstein evaluated every physical theory that came to his attention by his standard of oneness. He looked *through* things to see what they revealed about the deeply hidden, and so placed the issue of oneness in charge of his life work. That this led to his manifesting extraordinary intelligence demonstrates the validity of his orientation in life. That is what is important to us here.

Unlike Jesus, Einstein was not himself the subject of his scientific research on unity. He was not so concerned with his own being as a manifestation of the deeply hidden reality. Jesus was! Situation by situation Jesus placed his own life on the test point of oneness. Letting go of all usual supports, he relied only on underlying oneness. Anything inconsistent with oneness, he doubted. Anything consistent with oneness, he trusted. In this way he willingly gave the deeply hidden full sway over himself and those who trusted him. The outstanding wisdom, love, peace, and healing that followed brought to light and proved the truth and goodness of the deeply hidden on which he relied. Through his one-pointed consciousness the underlying mind or mindedness at the heart of life was able to act more freely and thus to manifest its intelligent, good, loving nature more fully.

Einstein's example and Jesus' example and exhortations demonstrate the desirability of focusing on and entrusting our lives to an invisible underlying force rather than to surface connections. What Einstein saw from his standpoint of oneness made him appear unusually intelligent. What Jesus saw made him not only unusually wise, but also unusually loving and healing. That he recommended detachment to us is another indication that he wanted *and thought possible* the same for us. He knew that we and our Father are one, too!

Children readily demonstrate the wisdom of the insecurity we have been considering. Two passages from Willa Cather's *My Antonia* illustrate. An orphaned child is sent West, ripped away from his world, which itself is coming apart. Traveling in the night, he peers out of the covered wagon.

There was nothing but land: not a country at all, but the material out of which countries are made. . . . I had the feeling that the world was left behind, that we had got over the edge of it, and were outside man's jurisdiction. I had never before looked up at the sky when there was not a familiar mountain ridge against it. But this was the complete dome of heaven, all there was of it. I did not believe that my dead father and mother were watching me from up there; they would still be looking for me at the sheep-fold down by the creek, or along the white road that led to the mountain pastures. I had left even their spirits behind me. The wagon jolted on, carrying me I knew not whither. I don't think I was homesick. If we never arrived anywhere, it did not matter. Between that earth and that sky I felt erased, blotted out. I did not say my prayers that night: here, I felt, what would be would be.[25]

But only half a dozen pages later he is completely at home in a new goodness, replanted and happier than ever in this bigger world, leaning against a warm yellow pumpkin in his grandmother's garden.

The earth was warm under me, and warm as I crumbled it through my fingers. Queer little red bugs came out and moved in slow squadrons around me. Their backs were polished vermillion, with black spots. I kept as still as I could. Nothing happened. I did not expect anything to happen. I was something that lay under the sun and felt it, like the pumpkins, and I did not want to be anything more. I was entirely happy. Perhaps we feel like that when we die and become a part of something entire, whether it is sun and air, or goodness and knowledge. At any rate, that is happiness: to be dissolved into something complete and great. When it comes to one, it comes as naturally as sleep.[26]

The child doesn't yet "know" enough to resist the force that governs and guides him from one goodness to the next. He hasn't yet been fooled by his senses into practicing the impractical practice of trying to run his own life and prove himself in relation to others. So he shows us what the great scriptures teach, which is that *there is something we can trust.* Our superficial perspective has fooled us all into seeking security by hanging on to certain interpersonal conditions and experiences in what is after all an exploding universe of divine self-revelation. This places us in opposition to the current of life and prevents us from increasingly seeing and expressing the unfolding good of God. But we too can learn to go with and be carried along by the flow—from one liberating revelation of the great eternal One to the next.

9. Universal Firsthand Realizations of Oneness

In inexperienced infancy
  many a sweet mistake doth lie:
A seeming somewhat more than view,
  That doth instruct the mind
  In things that lie behind
And many secrets to us show
  Which afterwards we come to know.
                    THOMAS TRAHERNE

At first a childhood, limitless and free
of any goals. Ah sweet unconsciousness.
Then sudden terror, schoolrooms, slavery,
the plunge into temptation and deep loss.

Defiance. The child bent becomes the bender,
inflicts on others what he once went through.
Loved, feared, rescuer, wrestler, victor,
he takes his vengeance, blow by blow.

And now in vast, cold, empty space, alone.
Yet hidden deep within the grown-up heart,
a longing for the first world, the ancient one . . .

Then from His place of ambush, God leapt out.
                    RAINER MARIA RILKE

Only a few decades ago, in New Guinea, a tribe of aborigines formed a "cargo cult." Having seen cargo planes flying overhead, the aborigines, too, wished to fly. In this hope they built a large airplane of trees and branches. It looked like a plane, but it was not a plane and did not fly. The aborigines worshiped and kept twenty-four-hour vigil beside the airplane. Through faithful devotion they hoped to persuade the gods to give them power to fly as well—to make their plane work or to give them a plane that would. Why had the gods empowered the city white people to defy the laws that kept them earthbound? When would the gods realize their oversight and raise them up, too? Torches were kept burning around the plane day and night so that the gods would notice them waiting in the woods. It did not occur to them that the laws they experienced as binding them to the earth were the same laws relied on by the flier to fly.

Throughout the world there is a cult around a man who rose above fear and hatred and death, who lived and loved on a higher plane. Everywhere people have tried to act like Jesus. In his name we have lived in poverty, "helped" our fellow humans mercilessly, martyred each other. It has never worked. It could not work any more than the aborigines' "airplane" could fly. Laws fly the plane. Law flew Jesus. Only reliance upon law can fly us.

There must have been a time when human beings did not know how to swim. So there must have been one who first discovered that swimming was possible. Did he not seem to break the law? Did he not seem an exception to the law—a powerful, magical person, perhaps a god, or at least one especially chosen by God?

People probably came from miles around and said, "Come see the amazing unsinkable man!" And perhaps he said, "I am not breaking the law; I am fulfilling it. It is not I who am doing the floating but the sea beneath that lifts me up. He who hath seen me afloat hath seen underlying buoyancy made manifest. I and the water are one in buoyancy." He might even have said, "The floating that I do shalt thou also do, and even greater feats shalt thou do because I have discovered and manifest this oneness." And we have done, and we do.

We have tried to act like Jesus, yet we have not loved or lived or healed. We are waiting for God or Jesus to make us whole and loving. But the floater can only float insofar as he realizes his own oneness with buoyancy. We are essentially seeing beings. "The son can do only that which he seeth the father do."[1]

And Peter answered him and said, Lord, if it be thou, bid me come unto thee on the water. And he said, Come . . .[2]

Einstein and Jesus staked their lives not only on the idea that there was a fundamental, reliable oneness, but also that it could be realized—which implies that it is idea (1) or spiritual in nature, perceivable. To say that we can realize it is also to say that through consciousness we are ourselves one with it. Through awareness we have something to do with this fundamental oneness, are a part of it. Our very yearning for oneness is our prescience of it. Einstein manifested it. Jesus realized it. What Einstein conceived of as the fundamental intelligibility of reality was cognized by Jesus as Fundamental Mind or God; and in realizing his own oneness with it Jesus recognized it finally as his Parent—the true source and force of his being, from whence his life came and on which he could rely for everything necessary to live it.

These men were not so much mental giants as places of enormous receptivity to a force beyond the self. As the compass is not smart but guided, as a wave is not a strong water-thing but an eruption of the sea beneath, so in these breakthrough individuals we find not enormous personal intelligence, but huge individual waves of underlying truth, God heaving himself up, reality bubbling up to the surface through their open consciousnesses. These living revelations of an underlying universal mind took place through a certain high level of deep-seeing, which we can call conscious oneness or oneconsciousness.

Only awareness of our oneness with the whole can heal us of the nightmare of separateness and the fear, pain, and frustration arising from it. Only awareness of our oneness with a guiding force beyond the self can free us from the anxiety of trying to be on our own and the hurt of relying overmuch on others. This alone can make us truly intelligent, peaceful, well, loving, spontaneous, and free.

So now we seek conscious oneness, or *oneconsciousness*. It is not enough just to know about, desire, or even to believe in oneness. Paul Tillich said, "There is no faith without understanding."[3] But even understanding is not enough. Although realization of oneness takes place in consciousness, it cannot take place in an armchair alone. You have to put your life on the line, to "lose your life to find it." Jesus tells us, "He that seeketh his own life shall lose it; but he that loseth his life for my sake shall find it."[4] It is an awesome threat and promise! He reassures us with evidence from nature:

Consider the lilies of the field, the birds of the air . . . they neither toil nor spin nor gather into barns, and yet your heavenly father feeds and clothes them. . . . If God so clothes the field . . . how much more will he clothe and feed you. Therefore take no thought for what ye shall eat, neither what ye shall put on . . . but seek ye first the kingdom and his righteousness, and all these things shall be added unto you.[5]

To give up taking thought for our lives? To entrust the master-minding of our lives to an intelligent force beyond ourselves, which we do not even know is there? This is hard. "If only I won't be alone . . . if only I'll be secure . . . if only he, she, they. . . ." If we give up taking thought for ourselves, who will look out for us? Alcoholics Anonymous says, "Let go and let God." But let go—how? Trust what?

Actually we know more than we think we do. Anyone who has learned to walk, talk, float, or to ride a bike has had realizations of oneness. Each represents the discovery of something beyond self and other that guides and governs things together for good. To walk we had to discover our own direct oneness with an invisible supportive force. By letting go of everything we had clung to and running the risk of falling flat, we discovered and realized our oneness with the underlying force and were able, ever after, to walk. By so trusting and risking we went from a time when no matter what we did everything was out of control to a oneness wherein, with next to no effort, we are protected, supported, guided, and freed by something *beyond the self*.

Someone may say, "Well, but the forces in walking and floating are physical and easily verified. What have they to do with our oneness with some invisible mind or God that I don't even know is there? There is no comparison." Yet we didn't know so much when we learned to float either. And the seeming risk was at least as great. We know how before it seemed so impossible and scary, how afterward it is really so easy and wonderful.

We are born buoyant. As the compass is one with the earth in magnetism, we are one with water in buoyancy. At least we have that capability. We cannot recognize our buoyancy by looking in the mirror. It is not visible, it is not self-contained; but rather it is something between us and the water. We also cannot discover it by objectively studying the water. At first our senses told us that water was a life-threatening, sinking, annihilating place. We got water up our noses, sucked in gulps of it, were sinking, couldn't breathe, desperately needed something to hang onto. It was only natural to fight against the water. All the time the water would have held us up, yet we were nearly drowning. In defending ourselves against the water, we also physically and mentally fought against the very buoyancy that would otherwise have held us up.

The admonition to "judge not by the appearance" (by the senses) applies to floating as to everything else in life.[6] As long as we were mentally preoccupied with sensory experience, buoyancy could not come to our attention. So, in both meanings of the word, buoyancy could not *occur* to us. We could not become aware of it, therefore it could not happen. But eventually, having learned to dog-paddle, we gave up dog-paddling. Having depended on parents or water wings, we let go of them. We gave up reliance on superficial-seeing for deep-seeing, connection-making for connection-seeing. Preoccupation with self-preservation was replaced by a willingness to entrust ourselves to an invisible force beyond the self. We had to lose our life to find it.

Consciousness

Anyone who has learned to float (not merely to swim) can recognize the primacy of consciousness in floating. Letting go is not enough. It is not enough to spread your arms and legs out rigidly or to relax limply. When you float, you consciously "feel after" buoyancy. This is not just physical. It involves awareness. Attention has to be paid. Once we learn to float, if we ever lose our oneness with buoyancy, we notice and immediately seek to recover it. We have "no other gods before" buoyancy. In such activities as walking, floating, riding a bike we do fulfill the first commandment—that is, we value oneness with the invisible governing force above all else. Our buoyancy becomes manifest when physically and mentally we let go of everything and rely only on buoyancy for support. It is through our conscious reliance on it that buoyancy actually becomes a supporting force.

What has changed? Only the content of consciousness. Only when buoyancy occupies our awareness can it gain its way with us. Arms and legs relax to just the right degree; breathing conforms; the waves no longer threaten. We are afloat—buoyancy incarnate! Oneness is a matter of awareness. When it occurs to us that it is so, it occurs as an event, a coming forth in experience. Thy kingdom come, thy will be done, in experience as it is in reality. This sequence is spelled out by John: "In the beginning was the word; and the word was with God; and the word was God; and the word became flesh and dwelt among us—full of grace and truth."[7]

So Peter got out of the boat and walked on the water and came to Jesus: but when he saw the wind, he was afraid, and beginning to sink he cried out, "Lord save me." And immediately Jesus reached out his hand and caught him, saying to him, "O man of little faith, why did you doubt."[8]

What actually took place is not so important as the story's meaning. It depicts a moment of oneness—its coming and its going. When Peter briefly walked on the water, inspired by Jesus' demonstration, he must have thought, "This is impossible! I can't do this; I'm too heavy. This is impossible!" That's when he sank. The point is that when he lost awareness of oneness, he also lost the proof of it.

Floating is analogous to and a step toward the larger task of realizing our oneness with God or Fundamental Mind. There is something beyond and beneath us that we can become aware of and depend on. Walking, floating, riding, talking—all these small steps for humankind, which were such big steps for each of us, took place exactly as those big steps for humankind taken by Columbus, Einstein, and Jesus. Now, as we seek even further spiritual awakening, we are not asked to do other than we have done before.

You say, "Not everyone can float! Some people sink!" But I say, "No, everyone can float; it is only that we do not all come to it so easily." I am delighted to tell you that I was once a sinker. Everyone said so. From Beginner to Water Safety Instructor, I passed every Red Cross requirement on every level, except floating. I was always excused from floating because it was clear that I was congenitally unable—a "vertical floater," or, more frankly, a "sinker." When I "floated," by craning my neck strenuously I could just keep my nose above water, but only my nose. Although I started in a horizontal position, within seconds I would be hanging vertically with only my nostrils sticking up. For me to pass any floating test it was necessary for the water to be deep enough so my feet wouldn't touch bottom, and calm—no wind, waves, or splashing.

Until Miss Schwarz. Miss Schwarz was my college swimming instructor—a small, hunched over, gray-haired woman in a short terry-cloth robe whom nobody remembered ever seeing in the water. The only evidence of her amphibiousness was a certain froggy appearance and a tendency to hoarseness—a perpetual frog in the throat. "Nonsense," she croaked. "You can float— and you will." After one session with Miss Schwarz, I floated. How she taught me is not important. I only know that, whereas for eighteen years I sank, ever since my encounter with Miss Schwarz I float. If I floated any higher, I could sit up and read. There is no effort or strain. It is nothing I do. But there is this force that I am finally aware of. It floats me. So don't tell me you can't float, because I will say, "Nonsense." And I know. To claim you can't float is like saying only Columbus could sail beyond the horizon, and that anyone else who tried would fall off.

The Letting Go Prayer

We all yearn to be at one—with each other, with life. Alone and seemingly on our own, we are fearful about what will become of us. When we try to use each other for support, we sink, struggling to be on top of or to get out from under each other.

But as much as we blame others and justify ourselves (or look up to others and blame ourselves), deep down we know better. Like children who instantly know it is not good to get water up the nose, we know it is not right to be at odds with each other or out of sync with life. At the same time that, coughing and choking, we violently object to water up the nose, we sense and yearn to realize the possibility of floating. Even as we stand spluttering and glaring at each other, we already sense and yearn to realize the possibility of being in love.

Floating is one thing. But we also have to realize our buoyancy in life, and perhaps beyond life, sailing beyond horizons of youth, career, marriage—even at last of body and space and time. We do not know what will happen beyond any horizon, least of all this last one. So, naturally, we hang back. But so far each letting go has brought greater security and freedom. Then perhaps we can learn to face each fear, every transition, even death—not in fear flailing, but in grace gracefully and grate-fully, not as a final sinking, but the next floating beyond the next horizon.

As I waited with my mother for the moment of her death, I was struck by many things. To her, God was meaningless. That there was somewhere a powerful, invisible God person seemed cold and unbelievable; yet mind or force was too abstract and nothing she could warm up to either. But as remaining alive and desperately ill became increasingly intolerable, she found herself considering God as an unturned stone beneath which she had not looked for help in dying. "Why can't I die?" she asked. "Why is it taking so long? What is holding me back?" We spoke of our tendency to hang onto the familiar, no matter how unpleasant, when afraid of the unknown. Otherwise what could I say? What did I know? Nothing. So I said nothing. I just sat beside her—letting go of my longstanding desire that she should love me (along with my longstanding impression that she didn't), in si-lent prayerful acknowledgment that God could reach her directly and did not depend on me to say the right thing—that there was no point at which anyone was ever out of God's reach—letting us both go into God.

One day toward the end a minister came to call. In the course of their brief visit, he mentioned Jesus' statement, "Into thy hands I commend my spirit."[9] Directly after, my mother called me in to say "something important." She repeated what the minister had said and how it had struck her. God as a person still had no meaning for her, but now she had a new idea. "I am substituting your words for 'God,'" she said.

I waited, wondering what words she had chosen. Love? Intelligence? "I am substituting 'let go' for 'God,'" she said. "It's very helpful. Isn't it good, Poll?"

"Very," I said, awed.

For two days, each time I saw her she repeated, "Let go, right? I am praying the letting go prayer. It won't be long, will it?"

I told her I was praying the letting go prayer, too, agreeing, "It won't be long now."

And it wasn't.

I puzzled over the choice of "let go" for "God." I think what she must have understood was that there was something to let go *into*. In beginning to recognize that, she was able to let go of her self at last, to stop fighting and relax into God—like a young child, finally floating.

Several years later I came across a poem written by my father's sister about his sitting beside their mother's bed as she lay dying. The language of letting go and water was startlingly similar to my written reflections on what had happened at my mother's bedside. I have two thoughts about this. One is that there is something universal going on here. (And, O, my beloved fellow aboriginal airplane cult worshipers, is this not what we see in every glorious stained glass window by Marc Chagall?—all of us floating, soaring in a beautiful blue Beyond?) The other is that letting go of each other and learning to float are somehow a major task of everyone in my family tree. Here is my aunt's lovely poem, which I read in 1989 at my father's funeral.

Dimittit

He talked his mother down to death,
Sitting by her bed in her dark room,
Holding her cold hand in his warm one.
Life was a long habit to her;
She'd been a cruelly long time dying.
Now he found courage
To ease her toward death
As she had released him, lovingly,
Long ago, to life.

She was a small skiff
Caught on the last reef
At the edge of the current's flowing.
He tried to be a tide for her
To float her over the dark undertow
Of coma and free her into the flood
Of the final unknowing.
"Let go, now, Mother. Let go," he said,
His voice gentle.
(She had always been afraid of deep water.)
"Don't hold on. Don't be afraid.
Let go—let go—"

Perhaps she heard.
Perhaps she knew.
Perhaps it was all she needed.
An hour later, when the family returned,
He was in tears.
He had succeeded.[10]

Fly, Grandmother! Fly, Mother! Fly, Father! Fly, Husband! Fly, my two dear brothers and beloved sons!

The Intruder

As children we made such rapid progress in discovering our oneness with certain invisible laws. Life drew us to itself, and we yielded joyfully, open-armed, open-eyed. In every case we first experienced each invisible law as chaos and confusion. As babies we were bombarded by strange noises and sensations, strange lights and colors, and flying appearances and disappearances. When we tried to stand, doors, floors, and furniture attacked us. When we tried to swim, the water invaded us. When we tried to ride a bike, it fell. We felt confused and got hurt. There was no sign of order or goodness here, nothing we had in common with the outside world. No oneness! Yet in an amazingly short time we discovered the order, meaning, and goodness beneath the chaos, and so mastered language, learned to read, walk, swim, ride, sing, move about, and find our way in an almost unbelievable variety of circumstances, and with the most wonderful freedom and ease! Oneness. Unwittingly we proved that "all things work together for good to them that love God."[11]

Recently it has been discovered that infants, unlike older children, take to water like ducks. Gently introduced to water, they do not gulp, panic, and thrash themselves into exhaustion. Rather, at least to some extent, they enter into rapport with the water, moving and floating responsively. They are not at all aware of buoyancy as such, but encountering it as a force, they soon find their oneness with it.

When did this rapid one-ing process slow down? What is the difference between infant water baby and scared, shivering, blue-lipped six-year-old? The degree of *self-consciousness.* Like Adam before the apple, the infant is relatively unself-conscious, whereas the six-year-old is already looking out for his mind-in-body. The things we learned with the greatest ease were not necessarily the easiest, but rather the earliest. Before we were preoccupied with self in the eyes of others, there was more room, more silence, for the still small voice of *what is* to be heard. There was simply not yet that much self to lose.

I have a vivid memory of my son that symbolizes how children are helped to change the subject of their lives from learning what's next to proving themselves.

At one year old he always came so fresh from his nap—all new and warm and flushed—smiling, bright and lovable with cherry red lips and fatfolds over his wrists. Still leaning too far forward, he toddled forth pell-mell to see what was next. We thought his entry so spectacularly cute that one day somebody jovially announced it with a cry of *ta da!* It was even cuter when he took to saying *ta da!* himself. We liked it that he thought of himself as a good thing worth a little fanfare. But when he was in his highchair and couldn't leap into the room himself, he would hurl other things—spoon, food, cup, dish—across the room, gleefully crying *ta da!* and waiting for everyone to be pleased. For a time there we were all leaping about: because whenever he said *ta da!* we knew something was going to get thrown. It was harmless, humorous, inevitable, but looking back we can see—he came from his sleep to see what's what, and we said to him, *"You* are what's what." One confusion leads to another.[12]

As children, until by way of personal approval (ta da!) and disapproval (tsk tsk!) we became self-conscious, we were almost pure awareness—receivers and transmitters of whatever was making itself known, to us and through us. We looked for oneness and it found us. I overheard my four-year-old talking his way through a picture book about frogs. He kept flipping back and forth through the pages. "Hmmm," he said (flip flip). "Frogs are bald. . . . All frogs are bald. . . . Frogs are all bald . . . (flip flip) . . . *All frogs are all bald!"* Oneness.

In the beginning almost every child makes the mistake of saying, "I amn't." Actually the English language makes the mistake because it OKs *can't, don't, isn't,* and *aren't,* but not *amn't.* So the child is not breaking the rule; it is the rule that breaks. The interesting thing is that children do search out the rules, which is to say they look for order, which is to say they look for unity—oneness! In the beginning it is all cacophony, but they listen through the chaos for the hidden order, the soundless unity, until they find, comply, and become one with it. And in no time at all, language is theirs. Nobody really sits down and teaches them all the complicated rules of English. Yet somehow they discover them.

Beyond Grown-Up

No wonder Jesus said, "Except ye become as a little child, ye shall not enter the kingdom of heaven."[13] We have to become like that again, openly approaching everything for the learning, always looking for the oneness. Whether in families or alone, at home or at large, in youth or old age—in order to float in life we need to stop hanging on (to self, other, thing, and circumstance) for support and defending ourselves against what is really a force of infinite intelligence and love. Perhaps exhausted, possibly sick and dying, we need to trust that there is something to let go into and therefore no need to hang onto anything. According to D. T. Suzuki, "Childlikeness has to be restored with long years of training in the art of self-forgetfulness."

The self is an intruder in consciousness. It is *the* intruder that comes between us and our oneness. Sometimes it is almost a total eclipse. What we need is to see beyond our selves. We cannot simply stop being self-conscious, but we can *lose* our self-consciousness in oneconsciousness.

When my mother was a little girl learning to swim, someone must have said, "It's all right, Mary. Lie back and relax. Let go. Don't worry. The water will hold you up." And eventually she did and it did. There is no end to the dying—and no end to the birthing.

Truly, truly I say to you, unless one is born anew, he cannot see the kingdom of God. . . . Truly, truly I say to you, unless one is born of water and the spirit he cannot enter the kingdom of God. That which is born of the flesh is flesh, and that which is born of the spirit is spirit.[15]

A Word of Hope

Our struggling has made us mistrustful. When we find we can't go it alone in life and our efforts to rely on each other bring us to hatred and double drowning, we infer that there is no good, no order, no God. But it is only that we are not obeying the laws. There are upholding forces that we are opposing. All our struggles are self-drownings. We try to use each other to stay on top of a seemingly alien milieu, a void. In truth, it is not a void, but God—with which, in reality, we are one; and in which we could float securely and frolic freely together if only we understood how to let it uphold us. Letting go *of* is so hard; letting go *into* is so wonderful. Onederful!

We do not have to wait until death to learn to let go. I have noticed that *I can trust God as far as I can trust him.* I find that the Red Sea parts as soon as, but not before, I set foot in it. The ground stops falling from under our feet after we stop running. We find God holding us up after we stop depending on anything else. We have more to go on than we realize. There are those buoyant ones before us—Buddha afloat on a water lily, Jesus walking on the water. And each of us has personally met some unsinkable ones, living saints upheld from below by something invisible that frees them to love—peaceful, unafraid, unstruggle-some almost, no matter what. Though waves rise up around them, they find calm. When death threatens, they remain in touch with life. Where sickness terrifies, they bring comfort, hope, and healing. Best of all are our own firsthand realizations that at least some of what we deem evil is not rooted in reality. That at least some of the bad things that happen, like water up the nose, noise in the ears, and bumps on the forehead, can be transcended through realization of oneness with invisible laws.

So we come to where we want to shift from the struggle to maintain separate whole selves to seek instead realization of our individual oneness with the whole through oneconsciousness. This is the turning point of this book and the turning point of our lives. We have yearned for it since Adam, with whom began the drowse and terror of not belonging, of having once belonged and longing to belong again. Jesus' realization of oneness is a proclamation of indestructable belonging that is not for the earning, but for the awakening. We, too, are invited beyond the parent/child, life/death struggle and catch-22 of always trying to go it alone in order to regain the right to be taken care of again. So it is that the nightmare of "grown-up" comes to an end as the child of God wakes up. So it is that Paul wrote, "For as in Adam, all die; so also in Christ shall all be made alive."[16]

Stages of Consciousness

Each life is a journey in consciousness. So far we have considered several stages of consciousness. The first is *unconsciousness,* in which reality is experienced largely through the senses. "Unconsciousness" is not precisely correct, for there is consciousness at this stage in the form of encounters with oneness, but we are unconscious of being conscious. It is really that we are un-*self*-conscious. This is epitomized by very young children and by Adam before the fall. It is/was pleasant enough. We can't really remember.

The second stage is *self-consciousness*. After a period of ignorant bliss, in which we experienced surface good through the senses, we all (by about age two) began to be aware of having ideas. With this "discovery" (spurred on by approving/disapproving parents) we entered self-consciousness. Still judging by the senses, we mistook the place where ideas occurred to us—our heads—for their source. So the self as a separate mind-in-body entity was conceived of and with it the whole troublesome business of trying to look after ourselves by growing up and, that failing, by making new interpersonal parental connections. *Self-consciousness* is characterized by increasing worry about the self—what it needs, what it wants, and how to get it. It could really be called *self/other*-consciousness because the inference made very early on is that our life support comes from, or at least depends on, others' approval. *Self-consciousness* is epitomized by Adam after the fall, and is the stage in which we have spent most of our lives so far.

But our separateness was not real, which is why connection-making has never worked. Our suffering, then, was neither punishment caused by an angry God, nor a sign that there is no God. It was not our failure and special wickedness, nor the failure or wickedness of others. It was only the experience of *mistakenness*. We have mistaken ourselves—road sign for road, compass needle for smart thing. Thinking we were minds-in-bodies, we have "taken thought," that is, we have taken over the thinking. What a *mis*-take. Our subsequent anxious exile, isolation, and suffering is only a side effect of the anxious babbling of our supposed minds, drowning out the "still small voice," the deeply hidden, inaudible but hearable, invisible but recognizable One Mind. Lack of depth perception is the only problem. As hard as it is to see the apple's connection to the tree, that skinny little stem, it is even harder to see our oneness with God. Because it isn't visible at all; it is spiritual. So it's harder to see; that's why we missed it. We are not alone.

The third stage is *oneconsciousness* or one-mindedness. We have begun to suspect that our suffering is not after all a sign of our special wickedness or worthlessness, nor of the nonexistence, lovelessness, or inadequacy of God. It is not a circumstance to change, but a dream from which to wake.

Deep-seeing is our only way out and the only thing lacking. It is simpler than we dream. Suppose you are driving a car. A bug smashes into your windshield and captures your attention. You continue to steer, but since you are not looking through the window at the road, you have nothing to guide you. Any second you will crash. But now you remember to look *through* the window instead of at it. Almost immediately harmony is restored. Understanding of what is intelligent occurs, intelligent behavior follows, and the tragic experience is healed before it happens. It all begins with viewpoint. Viewpoint determines what you see; what you see determines how you respond; how you respond determines what you experience.

When we look through the windshield at the road, we become one with the road. Now the road does the guiding, and guided, we respond intelligently. It is all a matter of oneconsciousness: the awareness of the presence of one underlying intelligence. This is epitomized by the lives of all the great spiritual guides. Oneconsciousness is characterized by a notable lack of self-concern and by the presence of unusual intelligence, peace, and love. Having seen evidence of oneness in the lives of others, we now seek to discover it firsthand. The way has been paved.

Jesus, Buddha, and Lao-tse were "oned" through conscious awakening. To realize our oneness we must assume the same at-one stance. So we seek to give up mentally hanging onto people and things to rely instead on something we can't see, or hear, but that can and does constitute and uphold our lives. We are looking for a mastermind of which everything, including ourselves, is a manifestation and by which we can be harmoniously and wonderfully governed if we give it a chance.

As self-consciousness is characterized by connection-*making*, oneconsciousness is characterized by connection-*seeing*. This is facilitated through contemplative and existential or living study and prayer, which are the means of cultivating spiritual consciousness over judgment by appearance. Reluctantly we tear ourselves away from our dreams, awaken, sit up, put our feet on the floor. What do you know! We are and have always been truly safe, embedded in God. Beautiful light is streaming in. A new day. Time to be up and about and in love.

I suppose there is a fourth stage of consciousness that is simply *consciousness*. Here the constant choice of what to pay attention to that characterizes oneconsciousness is replaced by pure awareness moment by moment of what is, and is manifest as love-inspired living. This is not as far out as it sounds. It must be similar to the point at which the toddler, having found his balance, no longer has to keep thinking about it. His oneness is established in consciousness, and he is free at last to move about safely and spontaneously. Gravity guides us when we walk. Magnetism directs the compass needle. The road steers the car. Through receptive awareness God, Fundamental Mind, "lives" our lives. We have all had glimpses.

10. The Need to Be Reminded

Now we are ready to look at something pretty special:
　　It's a duck riding the ocean a hundred feet beyond the surf.
No, it isn't a gull.
A gull always has a raucous touch about him.

This is some sort of a duck, and he cuddles into the swells.
He isn't cold, and he is thinking things over.
There is a big heaving in the Atlantic,
And he is part of it.

He looks a bit like a mandarin, or the Lord Buddha meditating under
　　the Bo tree.
　　But he has hardly enough above the eyes to be a philosopher.
　　He has poise, however, which is what philosophers must have.
He can rest while the Atlantic heaves, because he rests in the Atlantic.

Probably he doesn't *know* how large the ocean is, and neither do you.
But he *realizes* it.
And what does he do? I ask you. He sits down in it.
He reposes in it as if it were infinity—
　　which it is.

That is religion, and the duck has it.
He has made himself a part of the boundless, by easing himself
into it just where it touches him.

DONALD C. BABCOCK

Each childhood realization of oneness points not only to a fundamental law in its own sphere, but also to a fundamental intelligence, a Fundamental Mind, at the heart of all spheres, to God. Paul writes that to discover this presence and our oneness with it is the purpose of our entire life on earth. "If haply they might feel after and hopefully find him, though he be not far from every one of us, for in him we live and move and have our being."[1] We can test for Fundamental Mind by "haply" (through everyday happening) "feeling after" and basing our lives on it. It is there beneath all rough seas. In any situation we can discover and rely on its presence.

Conscious oneness is the key. Through it we overcome our

apartness and become assured, intelligent *participants* in life and loving *partners* with each other. For this to happen we need to see ourselves not as apart from but as part of Fundamental Mind. As buoyancy includes both buoying and buoyant aspects, as light includes both illumination and seeing, so the idea of mind includes both the generating and the awareness of ideas. Fundamental Mind thinks; we are meant to be aware. When we are aware of Fundamental Mind's ideas for us, we are truly guided and all is well. The trouble is we are rarely aware because, having mistaken the recipients of ideas for their source, we think we have to think.

To a baby the mother seems to be the source of nourishment, while in fact she is a conduit. Milk for the baby is formed within her body from nourishment she has taken in from the environment. Soon enough the child is weaned to feed more directly from the environment. The same is true with wisdom and love. The guidance and love initially delivered to the child by the parents are expressions of insight received by the parents. Ideally the child could (and to some extent does) grow in its capacity to process understanding directly from the vast intelligent environment of Fundamental Mind. But since as a species we have not yet completed our psychological weaning process, we continue to mistake *selves* for sources of wisdom and love. Thus the stumbling block of "grown-up," and with it the anxiety of looking out for ourselves and the hurt of not being able to rely on others. Still mistaking the receivers of God's ideas for the thinkers of them, we have the problem of at once *know*ing too much and almost never being *aware*.

The Willingness Not to Know

"How can you say I know too much when I am telling you I do not know enough! I am overwhelmed by my not knowing. I don't know what to do. I can't handle this situation." If you think the problem is that you don't know enough, then you are saying that you *should* know. And it is this *knowing* idea that is the problem to begin with. The serpent said, "When you eat of the fruit of the tree of *knowledge*, you shall be like God *knowing*." To us grown-up means, above all, knowing what's what and how to look out for ourselves.

Any employer can testify to the way employees disqualify themselves from jobs they could perfectly well learn to do if they didn't think they were already supposed to know. Any employee can testify to the misery of working for a boss who supposes he is the only one who knows what's what. Parents and children drive each other crazy with the idea that they are supposed to know.

Once I showed a youth group an unusual metal tool. Each tried, but no one could guess it was for pulling the reeds from a pump organ for cleaning. Asked what they would do if handed this tool and told to use it, they replied, "Ask what it's for." Now tougher questions were posed: "What are *we?*" and "What are we *for?*" A lengthy discussion ensued, with very little certainty and no consensus. So we uncovered the strange fact that although we set out each day to be and do the very best we can, we may never have asked, "What are we? What is an Andrew or Jan or Sarah or Rich or Allison?" We wouldn't try to use a tool without knowing its purpose, but we spend whole lifetimes trying to do a good job of being ourselves without asking, "What am I? What am I for?"

Like Adam, we answered these questions without asking them when we began to see ourselves as primarily thinking and knowing creatures. That's when we stopped being so receptive and began to be in over our heads, gasping for understanding, inadvertently fighting off inspiration.

The Illusion of Human Intelligence

In his later years, when India had become electric with his [Buddha's] message and kings themselves were bowing before him, people came to him even as they were to come to Jesus asking what he was. How many people have provoked this question: not "Who are you?" with respect to name, origin, or ancestry, but "What are you?—what order of being do you belong to, what species do you represent?" Not Caesar, certainly. Not Napoleon, nor even Socrates. Only two, Jesus and Buddha. When the people carried their puzzlement to the Buddha himself, the answer he gave provided a handle for his entire message.

"Are you a God?" they asked. "No." "An angel?" "No." "Then what are you?"

Buddha answered, "I am awake." His answer became his title, for this is what Buddha means. In the Sanskrit root *budh* denotes both to wake up and to know. Buddha, then, means the "Enlightened One" or the "Awakened One."[2]

There is a difference between *thinking and knowing* and *being aware*. It is the basic difference between Jesus, Buddha, and the rest of us. Buddha's knowing came through being awake. That is to say, he was aware. This is different from knowing or thinking. Buddha's knowledge was beyond him. But it came to him, and he was inspired by it, and so was formed by it as the wave is shaped by the surging sea.

We need to make a distinction between *think* as general mental activity and as generating thought. "I thought that up" implies that we have generated an idea. The idea that we think or know on our own is false. If your child tells stories "of her own" before she is old enough to go to school, you can see that she is just putting things together. All her stories are comprised of things that entered consciousness from without—experiences, books, shows, conversations. You know where every detail came from. When she goes to school, unfamiliar elements will suddenly appear in her stories. You may wonder, Hmm, where did that come from? But you will know it came from somewhere and was not something she truly "made up."

Our "knowledge" is the thoughts we have accepted as true. Our "thinking" is what we are doing with these thoughts. We may select from and synthesize thoughts, but even the standards we use in these thought processes are previously entered thoughts held onto as values. Many are thoughts about ourselves and others. The child of abusive parents may infer that *there is something bad about him that upsets people.* On the basis of this "knowledge," he concentrates on thinking of ways to correct this situation, and thus devotes his life to the false value of seeking approval. So we literally get "lost in thought." But we are never actually "thinking up thoughts." What we call thinking is just the processing of thoughts already entertained.

Entertainment is what captures attention and holds interest. We are always working with elements of thought that "entered" and got "tained" (from Latin *tenere, to hold*). There is a mutual holding of thinker and thought. Thought enters consciousness and captures attention, whereupon consciousness tends to hold onto the thought. As the driver of a car determines the car's course, the thoughts we entertain run our lives for ill or good. The question is, Are they true and deserving of our allegiance, or false and good for nothing? Are they erroneous inferences? or reliable inspirations from Fundamental Mind?

Fundamental Mind cannot guide and inspire us when we are trying to be "like God, knowing," any more than buoyancy can uphold us when we are not relying on it. It is like fake floating. There are two ways to stay on top of the water without truly floating: by dog-paddling and by hanging on. Figuring things out is mental dog-paddling (self-reliance). Trying to get others to cooperate, comply, agree, approve is mentally hanging onto them for support. Dog-paddling is lonely and exhausting. The hanging on way is full of conflict, hurt, frustration. Both ultimately lead to sinking. Realization that we are supported by Fundamental Mind depends not on our thinking and knowing, but rather on our becoming open and aware. As a puddle poured into the sea becomes a lively graceful wave, ever replenished, reformed, and revitalized with new surges of water, so when we reorient ourselves toward Fundamental Mind our lives are shaped by divine inspiration! We need to lose our mind to find it, to shut up and be *re-minded*.

Answers to Common Objections

A key issue in our actually relying on Fundamental Mind is trust. To trust Fundamental Mind, God, depends on whether or not we have any reason to believe that it exists, that it is good rather than evil, and that it will apply directly to us and our situation. Therefore, as much as we suffer from depending on self and other, certain major frightening questions arise whenever we consider entrusting ourselves to an unknown God, Fundamental Mind. Is it true? Is it good? Does it care about me? Before we move on to the matter of how to let go of our minds in order to discover our oneness with Fundamental Mind, it will be good to consider some common objections that often arise when these ideas are being presented.

Is It True?

Is it true? Is it good? What about all the evil in the world? What about people in the Third World? The most frequently raised objection is to the idea that wherever we suffer is where we have something to learn—that sometimes our sufferings are brought on by our errors—that always they have something to teach us—that if our problems do not arise from our error then at least they arise from our ignorance of God—that in any case God does not cause them. Many complain that this perspective denies the existence of evil, and therefore seems either Pollyanna-ish or heartless or both. "It's easy for you to say," they say. "You're healthy. You live in a free country. Your children aren't dying of starvation."

I have already dealt with this in a general way, but here I'd like to speak from a somewhat more personal standpoint. First of all, it is *not* easy for me to say. In the face of unthinkable crimes, genocide, autogenocide, sudden infant death, slow infant death, it is almost impossible to say. Even just in the face of my own suffering, whether from "real" or "imagined" causes, it is also not easy to say. But for the same reasons that it is not easy to say this, it is impossible *not* to say it—because *then what?* So then the question is, From what standpoint can it be said? Here are some of the reasons I can or have to speak as I do.

For one thing, I have found in every hard thing in my life some lesson that, once learned, seemed worth learning. Often enough to keep me going, this learning approach to suffering "works" not only in helping me learn something valuable but even in healing or at least ameliorating the immediate difficulty. Furthermore, every such realization seems to enable me to help others see through and transcend their difficulties. I have never seen a dead person come back to life or a limb grow back, but in counseling sessions I have seen chronic migraine headaches disappear on the spot, never to return again; I have watched people weeping and trembling and rocking back and forth on the verge of mental breakdown suddenly grow calm and reasonable and chuckle at themselves. I have known what it is to want to die rather than accept that I could not change something, only to find that when I yielded, either the unchangeable changed or I saw that it wasn't important. Even when it doesn't "work," it helps. Even if it wouldn't be true, this would still be the most practical, helpful, happy, sane, constructive way to approach one's problems in life.

As for global suffering, I see enough similarity between individual interpersonal difficulties and collective international ones to believe that they are not different. I do not believe it is reasonable to expect healing in collective arenas before there is healing on an individual level. I know that individual awakening is of direct and immediate benefit in the collective sphere.

As for innocent victims, I can only say that this is a mystery beyond my ken. But I have seen enough order where I formerly experienced chaos, and enough healing where I formerly experienced evil to infer that life is fundamentally orderly and good. I don't know what comes next, but maybe death *isn't* sad—except for those of us who are left behind, wanting to hang on and not knowing better. I also see that it is difficult to compare degrees of suffering—long term with short term, acute with chronic, physical with psychological. I am certain that spiritual awakening has to take place on an individual level, and that my individual awakening will be the best contribution I can make to my fellows, both at home and abroad.

The following passages from Wendell Berry's novel *Remembering* serve as illustrations of these thoughts. A farmer who has lost one of his hands in an accident, and with it all sense of life's meaning and value, has the following conversation:

It was as though he continued to speak to his hand, which did not answer. And this was a loss of speech that could not be spoken of to anyone still whole and alive.

He felt his father watching him, worried about him, and he shied away.

His mother gave him no chance to shy away. "Come sit here," she said, reminding him for the first time of her mother.

"Andy, I'm sorry for what's happened. I can't tell you how sorry. But you must learn something from it."

"Learn!"

"What you don't know, you'll have to learn."

"What?"

"I don't know. But you must accept this as given to you to learn from or it will hurt you worse than it already has."

He knew that she had missed nothing. He sat under her words with his head down as he had sat, when he was a boy, under a scolding. But she was not scolding.[3]

Later, as he begins to heal, many things from the past come back to help him. One is the following recollection told to him as a boy by Mat about when he was a boy.

"Boys," Mat says, "it was a *hot* day. There wasn't a breeze anywhere in that bottom that would have moved a cobweb. It was punishing." He is telling Elton and Andy.

It was a long time ago. Mat was only a boy yet, though he was nearly grown. His Uncle Jack hired him to help chop out a field of tall corn in a creek bottom. It was hot and still, and the heat stood close around them as they worked. They felt they needed to tiptoe to get enough air.

Mat thought he could not stand it any longer, and then he stood it a little longer, and they reached the end of the row.

"Let's go sink ourselves in the creek," Jack said.

They did. They hung their sweated clothes on willows in the sun to dry, and sank themselves in the cool stream up to their noses. It was a good hole, deep and shady, with the sound of the riffles above and below, and a kingfisher flying in and seeing them and flying away. All that afternoon when they got too hot, they went there.

"Well sir," Mat says, "it made that hard day good. I thought of all the times I'd worked in that field, hurrying to get through, to get to a better place, and it had been there all the time. I can't say I've always lived by what I learned that day—I wish I had—but I've never forgot."

"What?" Andy says.

"That it was there all the time."

"What?"

"Redemption," Mat says, and laughs. "A little flowing stream."[4]

As far back as I can remember, I have spent my life trying to prove to myself and to others that life is good. Many times I have asked myself, "Why do I insist that it is good?" Sometimes I think it is to overcome despair that would otherwise overwhelm. Sometimes I am sure it is God forcing itself to the surface. And I suppose that really is just what it is—redemption and grace!

Does It Care?

Does it care? I do not believe in a bearded, personal Father in heaven; but this idea of Fundamental Mind seems cold and indifferent. What good is a God that doesn't care about me personally? Surprisingly many "nonbelievers" are disappointed to hear the God they don't believe in spoken of in nonpersonal terms. They say, "If I'm going to believe in God, I want you to prove that God cares about me personally."

My question is, "What do you want from this personal God?"

Usually the answer is comfort, protection, guidance, companionship, and above all *love*. Of course these are what I yearn for, too. And they are what I am slowly discovering are provided for me, by a God that is beyond all personhood.

Before you learn to walk, you need others' support. But once you can walk an omnipresent force provides directly that enabling support and protection. No matter where you go, it is there, taking whatever shape is needed. Is this not love? Once you can walk you no longer need someone to hold you up, to say, "There, there" when you fall. When "others" are needed to guide, assist, or share the joy, they are there. But that, too, is part of the omnipresence, the love of Fundamental Mind, which takes shape as everyone and everything needed from one moment to the next.

Once, in prayerful preparation for a seminar, I found myself considering the question of what it is that is necessary from our end. The words *purify* and *obey* came to mind. I saw that we need only to purify our thoughts of every idea that contradicts the existence of God. Then, inevitably, Fundamental Mind presents us with a fresh, true idea. After that, I saw, what is needed is simply to obey whatever idea has come. Next, the words *living love* came to mind. I understood that the long-sought, unattainable love we all yearn for would be the inevitable result brought about by God if we followed through with our simple steps of *purify and obey.*

I was passing through a period of deep personal sorrow, so the next day when the same thoughts occurred to me in prayer I was again deeply attentive. I saw that I had been given a beautiful existential equation for living: Purify + Obey→ Living Love. It can be spelled out as follows.

1. *Purify.* In quiet prayer we free ourselves of habitual erroneous ideas and open ourselves to God's ideas for the living of this moment, which then immediately come.
2. *Obey.* In living prayer we bring our whole being—thought, word, deed, and entire way of conducting ourselves—into service of the idea we have just received from God.
3. *Living Love* takes place as the inevitable byproduct of alignment with and reliance on Fundamental Mind's ideas for us.

When these thoughts occurred to me I was alone in the car, which is when I am most likely to give vent to thoughts and feelings out loud. "Yes!" I shouted, acknowledging that this is all that is required and what will inevitably result, and that all we have to do is say yes. Moments later it crossed my mind that the prayer I had been given spelled my name: *P*urify-*O*bey-*L*iving-*L*ove-*Y*es. P-o-l-l-y! So it was brought home to me that not only was this *the* way, but also that it was my way, my life, what I am for—in fact, me.

You may say that this is corny. You may say that an idea of God that is not a person and has no personal feeling for me—neither pity, nor pride, nor warmth—is cold. But in that moment I felt, *knew,* that I was individually loved. Interpersonal it is not, yet it is very personal. That God is love, and that this love applies to each of us precisely and particularly, is a great mystery, a great *reliable* mystery.

Why Bother to Call It God?

Why bother to call it God? One reason is that it *is* God—and though it is not a personal God, it is very personal and particular in the way it meets our needs and in this way loves us. Another reason is that by using *God,* we open ourselves to a wealth of traditional inspired literature that suddenly comes to life when viewed in an existential light. So much of this is familiar to us that as we see how it is so, we find we already have much to go on. We discover that this wisdom is not just a set of beliefs, but scientific/existential discoveries made over and over by inspired seekers from all over the globe and throughout history going deeper and deeper into truth.

It is so wonderful to live in a time when we can actually hold in our own hands translations in our own language of mythological and religious scriptures from all over the world and from way back in time. Whether you are committed to a particular faith or are not at all sure of what you believe, I heartily recommend that you take time to explore this wealth. Wherever you stand, it can only deepen your understanding and decrease your loneliness. And afterwards Westerners, at least, will find in the Bible a very special source of guidance, encouragement, as well as the loving companionship of those who have suffered, sought, and seen before.

Part, Parcel, Partners, and Participants in Love

Our quest for love is the biggest reason for retaining the name God. Our tradition wisely tells us that "God is love."[5]

Whither shall I go from thy spirit?
Or whither shall I flee from thy presence?
If I ascend up into heaven, thou art there.
If I make my bed in hell, behold, thou art there.
If I take the wings of the morning,
and dwell in the uttermost parts of the sea,
Even there shall thy hand lead me,
and thy right hand shall hold me. . . .[6]

For I am persuaded that neither death, nor life, not angels, nor principalities, nor powers, nor depth, nor any other creature shall be able to separate us from the love of God which is in Christ Jesus.[7]

The more we enlarge our concept of God from a temperamental blowup of human parents to a reliable universal force, the more we recognize its manifold presence as love and, accordingly, the more loving we become. The more we learn to participate in Fundamental Mind by being receptive and aware, the more we find ourselves in loving partnership with others. As there are laws for walking, floating, and bike-riding, there are laws to facilitate human relationships, health, creativity. Fundamental Mind manifests itself in the loving meeting of all our needs. Through conscious oneness with Fundamental Mind love above, all abounds.

How often our plans together go sour! It seemed so simple, and yet suddenly we are angry. Someone feels left out, put down, railroaded. How did it get so complicated? We want to blame others and justify ourselves, but we sense this is not the problem—that we just haven't understood participation. It is not that love isn't, only that we aren't truly loving.

One woman enjoyed her visits to an elderly relative. Though physically weak, he was mentally alert, and she looked forward to lively discussions with him and the young man hired to keep him company. But one day she was amazed to hear the companion quote a famous physicist's esoteric theory. Within minutes she was overcome with lust and began to imagine she was falling in love with him. Being a married woman, she saw the impossibility of this fantasy and sought to free herself. In counseling she recognized in the episode her strong desire to be intellectually superior, especially over men. Initially she had enjoyed her visits as a chance to match wits in a "no contest" situation with a weak old man and his inferior servant. But once the young man's remark revealed his *very* keen mind, all that changed. Her ensuing lust was nothing more than envy, the desire to possess his mind or conquer it by winning his admiration. She saw that this idea of love was a travesty.

Many worry that reliance on God, instead of on others, will mean a loveless life. But, as this story illustrates, our usual idea of love is really a travesty of love in the form of envy and power struggle. The dictionary definition of *travesty* is *grotesque imitation*. Abandoning a travesty does not mean losing the real thing. In fact, it is only when we abandon our grotesque imitations of love that real love can begin. Spiritual consciousness is not the end but the beginning of love.

It is the basic confusion about mind that gives rise to our painful confusions about love. What we call love is the life support we think we have to wrest from others (and their willingness to let us do that). This is analogous to the ridiculous idea that a finger must either know how to read (self-reliance) in order to point to a specific word on the page, or win support from other fingers (other-reliance) to turn to the right page. Our fingers turn pages and point to words, but they cannot read. If they thought they had to read or to organize each other in cooperative efforts, they would be as desperate as we are about what to do and as manipulative about getting others' cooperation. But there is no such problem because, of course, everything the fingers need to care for them and put them to good use is being pumped out and transmitted to them. They know nothing, and yet, cooperating beautifully together, they thread needles, perform microsurgery, play violins, and write books.

In oneconsciousness we realize that we do not have to mentally possess or manipulate each other. So instead we learn to let Fundamental Mind guide everyone, beginning with ourselves. This alleviates mutual fear and conflict. "The eye cannot say to the hand, 'I have no need of thee.'"[8] Both are needed—eye for seeing, hand for holding, finger for turning and pointing. The eye cannot turn pages; the finger cannot see letters. Neither can do its job without the other; neither can do the other's job. Yet neither really does its own job either. Without the brain the hand is paralyzed, the eye blind. Each is guided and enlivened by a reality beyond itself. It is through eye and hand that the mind sees and reads. It is through both you and me that God expresses what God is and accomplishes what God has in mind. So the Bible does not say, "Off *them* I live and move and get my being," but "In God we live and move and have our being."[9] When we learn to participate individually in Fundamental Mind, we become at last partners in love.

One man I worked with enjoyed the hobby of music, playing and singing in various amateur groups. At a time of considerable spiritual awakening, he heard of a new voice teacher. In their very first lesson the new teacher uncovered in him tremendous singing power and beauty of which he had never been aware, even though he had been singing all his life. "Isn't it wonderful?" he told me joyfully. "He was so enthusiastic about my voice that he wanted me to come more than once a week at first! But of course I told him I couldn't afford that."

"*What?*" I exclaimed. "Here is life trying to give you your fulfillment, and you say, 'That's nice, but I can't afford it'?"

He quickly recognized the fallacy in his profession of lack. For so long he had been working to become God-reliant rather than people-reliant. The opportunity to study with the fine teacher had sprung up out of the blue, an unwished wish come true. But even in the moment of receiving this gift, fear of letting go of his ability to take care of himself (his money) and desire to be taken care of by somebody else had tempted him. He had chosen to switch from the context of God back to the context of self and other, hinting that he lacked, trying to set up a child/parent dependency on the teacher, to get the teacher to come down in price, or perhaps give him some free lessons. Instead of participating joyfully with the teacher in the divine business of music making, he had tried to use the lessons as a means of extorting personal support from the teacher.

"Have you got enough money for an extra lesson this week?" I asked.

"Yes," he said.

"And next week?"

"Yes!"

"Then for goodness' sake, claim your inheritance as a child of God!"

Having clearly recognized his error and his opportunity, the man went off eagerly to make an appointment for an extra lesson. The next day, again from "out of the blue," he was introduced to the friend of a friend, who happened to be the music director of a large urban cathedral. During their meeting, the music director invited him to sing for her. She was so impressed that she hired him to be the soloist for the next service and to replace her as music director the following four weeks while she was away on vacation! "Eye hath not seen, nor ear heard, the things that God hath planned for those that love him."[10]

One couple could never make decisions together. They suffered constant disagreements over what was best and often feared that things would not work out because one of them was wrong. Fear of conflict and of making the wrong decision was always present. Eventually they saw that they were like contestants. No matter what the topic—whether planning a trip, having guests, or managing finances—it became a game board for their contest of mental supremacy. Your move. My move. The real fear was not so much over what would happen as of being wrong—of losing the game and being "wiped out." Now they prayerfully considered the idea that God is the only mind, and that therefore there was no need to confirm their own mental power or fear the power of others. Soon thereafter they were traveling on vacation in unfamiliar territory with indefinite plans. When the familiar fear over decisions arose, they continued to pray. Repeatedly the thoughts, "This is God's idea" and "God only knows" came to mind, bringing surprising peace. It was their best vacation since their honeymoon, and they said they were falling in love again.

Asking: The Difference That Makes the Difference

Once we recognize the importance of the thoughts we entertain, we aspire to let only thoughts from Fundamental Mind run our lives. This is the purpose of prayer. Now we see why prayer is extremely important and why Jesus said, "Pray without ceasing."[11]

To pray means to ask. It is not necessary to ask specific questions, only to be open, interested, and willing. Prayer asks simply, What is so? In so asking we momentarily let go of habitual previously entered thoughts, especially the idea of taking thought, open up to Fundamental Mind, and are "re-minded." This is the real losing of life—by letting go of one's mind (and its mindings) in order to find it—by letting go into Fundamental Mind. Prayer is our way of letting go of, and letting go into.

An actress was called at the last minute for an audition. She did not want to take her young son along, because he didn't like to be left in the waiting room; but he was very restless and distracting if allowed to be present during the audition. She began to feel irritated at being called so late and resentful that it always fell to her to either care for her child or find a sitter. As she prepared to leave, it occurred to her that she could not possibly do well in the audition in such a state. She took a moment to get quiet and seek prayerfully a more spiritual perspective on her situation. She realized it could not be possible for her gain to be her son's loss, or for his well-being to depend on her loss. Either he would be happy in the waiting room, or she would find a sitter. Either things would work out fine, or she would learn something.

When she did not find a sitter after a few calls, she set out peacefully with her son. At the studio, when her call came, she reassured her son that she would be right back. But to her surprise the producer invited him in, too. "It's all right," said the mother. "I'm sure he'll be fine right here." "Yes," said the producer, "but I would like him to participate in the audition. You are to play a mother with a child in her lap." Instead of having to pretend she was holding a child, she did the scene with her son in her lap. At the end of the scene, when she looked down at him and spoke the concluding words, "Right, honey?" her son looked up sweetly and smiled.

"Right, Mommy," he said.

We were never meant to know. We are meant to be aware of what Fundamental Mind knows, and only of what it is knowing in our way at this time. We can only be aware if we are listening. Not knowing. Not telling. Not thinking. Not calculating. But listening. Attending. Asking. Not trying to figure out what to do about the separateness, but seeking to be aware of the oneness.

11. False Prayer: Avoiding the Void

The Seal Lullabye

Oh! Hush thee, my baby, the night is behind us,
And black are the waters that sparkled so green.
The moon, o'er the combers, looks downward to find us
At rest in the hollows that rustle between.
Where billow meets billow, there soft be thy pillow,
Ah, weary wee flipperling, curl at thy ease!
The storm shall not wake thee, nor shark overtake thee,
Asleep in the arms of the slow-swinging seas!

RUDYARD KIPLING

A child was walking in the woods holding her father's hand. Everything was lovely. She just went along and observed each next wonderful thing without worrying what lay behind or before. But she fell asleep, and suddenly awoke to find him gone. She was alone and frightened.[1] Imagining all sorts of dangers, she ran blindly into things and hurt herself. In her panic, she startled other creatures, who growled and snapped at her in fear. Now, the woods were the same beautiful woods; but because she was on her own and didn't know where she was or what to do or what lay ahead, she reacted in such a way that she became lost and hurt and could only conclude that the woods were a terrible place. And she had all kinds of scrapes and bruises to prove it. In fact, for all we know, she may have been eaten by the big bad wolf.

A background premise behind all anxious thinking is the notion of a Great Out There, a mindless, careless milieu through which we have to navigate and against which we must protect ourselves. As infants we did not notice the importance of mind. But the minute her father disappears, the little girl becomes acutely aware of mind: She does not know the way. To her the forest is an alien place that can swallow her up. Now that she is aware of mind it is even worse, because if she looks at the woods for mind, she sees it as mindless. In being mindless of her, the woods even seem malicious—if not for her, against her. If her father would return, she would be relieved, because she trusts his mind and its knowledge. But even if she gets out of the woods alone, from now on she will struggle between the thought that she needs to, but does not know her way through life, and the impression that she must stay in contact with someone else who (she will keep finding) cannot be counted upon. So from now on she will want mental hand-holding as well as hand hand-holding.

Actually the forest is full of signs to guide her! The sun shines through the trees where the road home lies close by; the brook that bubbles through her own backyard babbles loudly ahead. Running headlong in the wrong direction she trips over the roots of a tree, from which her house can clearly be seen if she would only look. But she does not see the guidance. She does not hear the still small voice that whispers, "Fear not. . . . Be still and know that I am God. . . . In all thy ways acknowledge me, and I will direct thy paths."[2] Her father returns to where he left her sleeping only moments ago. But the little girl has gone looking for him.

As with the little girl in the woods, it is against the background of a mindless void that our desperation to look out for ourselves by making interpersonal connections arises. It is this myth of the malicious milieu that gives the myth of human intelligence such a headhold on us. From the moment we first thought with childish dread, *I don't know what's under the bed, I don't know where Mommy is, I don't know what will happen to me,* we have been aware of our dependency on mind. Since then, we have had it all backwards. We have seen our milieu as mindless and ourselves as having minds, while in truth our milieu is mind and we do not have or need separate minds of our own. We turn to prayer for freedom from this illusion. This beautiful hymn highlights what we are seeking to realize:

> In heavenly love abiding, no change my heart shall fear,
> And safe is such confiding, for nothing changes here.
> The storm may roar about me, my heart may low be laid,
> But God is round about me, and can I be dismayed?
>
> Wherever He may guide me, no want shall turn me back;
> My shepherd is beside me, and nothing can I lack.
> His wisdom ever waketh; His sight is never dim;
> He knows the way He taketh; and I will walk with Him.
>
> Green pastures are before me, which yet I have not seen.
> Bright skies will soon be o'er me where darkest clouds have been.
> My hope I cannot measure; my path in life is free.
> My Father has my treasure, and He will walk with me.[3]

True and False Prayer

Some say *prayer*, some say *meditation*, some say *prayer and meditation*. I use just *prayer*. If you aren't comfortable with this word, you can substitute "tuning in." When I pray, sometimes I am really tuning in, but sometimes I am just fussing and fretting and finagling. Sometimes when I think I'm praying, I'm not. Sometimes when I am not conscious of praying, I am. It is a question of motive and sincerity. At best, prayer is the way to become aware; at worst, it is just another attempt at knowing. At best it is spiritual, connection-seeing, and leads to realized oneness; at worst it is re-ligious, connection-making, and augments our apartness. In false prayer we seek supportive connections to defend us against the malicious mindless void. True prayer is the way to realize our oneness with omnipresent, loving Fundamental Mind.

In swimming, we have to give up physically hanging on to supports. In life, we have to give up mentally clinging, in order to prove to ourselves that what we thought was a mindless void is after all deep, supportive Fundamental Mind—in which we live and move and have our being. To so let go into oneness is the purpose of true prayer. But we cannot *do* it anymore than we ever *did* floating, because it is not done; it is discovered—first in viewpoint, then as understanding, then as participation, finally as realization, manifestation, or incarnation.

True prayer happens only when our yearning for oneness is so great that we are momentarily willing to drop our connecting strategies. We have already observed that connection-making is our primary occupation; now we must see that it is all we ever think about as well. Only when we recognize this obsession can we consider letting go of it. Suppose you slip on ice. Instinctively, you grab the person next to you, who happens to be an old woman. Instead of supporting you, she falls down. You fall on top of her, breaking her collarbone. A bunch of other people trip and fall over both of you. Obviously, it would have been better if you had maintained your center of gravity.

We experience many more troublesome interpersonal colli-sions without any recognition that we have been illegitimately hanging on to each other for support, which we could have been receiving from God. Had we any idea what tyrannical violence this mental connection-making is, we would have tried to give it up long ago. Yet connection-making is what we are thinking *and praying* about almost all the time.

It is important to recognize that not all praying is true prayer. Sometimes people ask, "Are you religious? I mean, confiden-tially, *do you pray?*" There is a belief that prayer is optional, oc-casional, and unusual. Most assume it is only for those who believe in God, which implies that it is not quite reasonable, or at least naive. So there is often embarrassment when prayer is mentioned. Actually, everyone prays most of the time. Unfortu-nately, it is mostly false prayer. The thoughts and intentions that give rise to our coping/connecting repertoires can be regarded as false, connecting prayers. The first thought behind both true and false prayer is, *I feel separate and unviable, therefore it is important for me to be connected.* In true prayer the feeling of separateness and unviability is recognized as an illusion to be overcome by *recognizing* our deep oneness with Fundamental Mind. False prayer assumes our separateness and endangerment to be real and is dedicated to *making* superficial supportive connections.

The dictionary defines *prayer* as petitioning, asking, or, we could say, expressing a desire. So after all, we rarely stop praying! False prayer isn't simply thinking; there is a worshiping, prayerful quality to it. In this sense, even when we brush our teeth we pray. We don't just brush. We look in the mirror and think of what we want and how to connect up to it: *If I can't brush this stain from my teeth, they won't like me. Maybe if I can brush this stain from my teeth, someone will like me better, vote for me, marry me . . .* We may be concerned with appearance or success, or what so and so said and what we wish we had said back or will next time. From admiration or compliance, to riches and pleasure, we are always mentally reaching for someone or something outside of ourselves with re-ligious fervor. So to ask, "Do you pray?" is like asking, "Do you breathe?" Scientists have identified a sleep phase characterized by rapid eye movement (REM). Even in sleep we are looking for something—seeking, praying.

Wishing is the simplest form of false, connecting prayer. For example, "I am dying for a cigarette" includes the reaching thought, "How can I get one?" In this sort of "octopus consciousness," we are continually sending out thought tentacles. Wishing, calculating, speculating, fantasizing, these mental tentacles mentally suction onto things. Into future and past we reach, to arrange and rearrange our relationships and experiences. The nonswimmer has only two arms and legs with which to hang on or wrap himself around things, the octopus only eight. But there is no limit to the mental tentacles ("mentacles") we put forth in our false prayers.

Another common shape that false connecting prayer takes is *waiting*. Waiting says, *My good life or my peace of mind will begin when/if a certain thing happens.* It denies God. It ignores the good life that is available to us now. I think it is one of our biggest sins. Certainly it is a widely committed one. I know it is one of mine.

It was one thing to acknowledge that the superior intelligence we observed in Jesus or Einstein was really not personal but from the mind of God. It is quite another to let go of our own albeit inferior but familiar and caring personal minds. It is very frightening to consider that we do not need to look out for ourselves. But either this isn't the case, or God isn't God.

Pitfalls on the Prayerful Path

Even if we pray to God, we may engage in false, connecting prayer. The tendency is to use God as the means of connecting to some thing, person, or result. *Dear God, please get this, change them, fix that,* we pray. God is not being worshiped here. God is just the connection. To worship God we would have to worship what God *is*, not just what God can get for us.

There is always an idea of human mental power behind these prayers. We try to connect with what we "think" we "know" is best. If we seem to succeed, we not only experience the desired feeling of connection, but also the comforting sense that we do indeed "know" best and have power to avoid the void. Often when we pray to God, our asking is really telling. We know what we want and are telling God to get it. There is a difference between question and request. True prayerful asking seeks understanding, whereas in requesting we are only trying to get what we want. In the first case, God is mind, and we are instrumental; in the second, we have minds for knowing and telling, and God is instrumental. We say, "Oh, yes, I pray. I asked God to help my wife. I asked him to make her understand my needs." We know and tell God what we think should be done. Referring to Samuel's response to God's call, it has been said that, "For one soul that exclaims, 'Speak, Lord, for thy servant heareth,' there are ten that say, 'Listen, Lord, for thy servant speaketh.'"[4]

Even prayers of praise and thanksgiving can have the ulterior motive of telling God what to do. When we refer to God as a higher intelligence, it is still only an *other* intelligence besides our own. Calling it "higher" may be just an ingratiating way of trying to influence it to do what we "know" is best. It may be indirect, but it is telling all the same. *Mine the kingdom, mine the power, mine the glory.*

If telling prayer does not lead to inspiration or healing, it is because it seeks neither. Turning to this type of prayer may be of some benefit just in getting us off others' backs, and in that we have fleetingly regarded our problems as something that can go away. A sense of possibility is always helpful. Into even the smallest credibility gap, God is ready to get a word in edgewise. Occasional good "results" of positive thinking and imaging demonstrate this phenomenon.

Another pitfall is pseudo-asking. So James said, "Ye ask and receive not, because ye ask amiss."[5] He did not say pray more, but pray otherwise. For example, there was a story of a professor who traveled overseas to study with a Zen master. "First have some tea," said the master, handing the professor an empty cup and saucer. He filled the cup to the brim, and kept pouring until the pot was empty and both student and floor were awash. The professor rose aghast, crying, "Watch out! What are you doing?" The master bowed, gesturing that the session was over. The professor departed, scratching his head.

The professor was proud of knowing. The teacup stood for the professor, the tea for the teaching. No tea could be poured into the full cup. To try was a waste. The professor asked but did not receive, because he asked amiss. He could not receive new understanding because he was already full of himself. He pretended to ask to see, but only wanted to seem to know. There was no point in meeting until he had more interest in learning than in already knowing, in seeing than in seeming.

Once I had a student without eyesight. In working together, we discovered that "real seeing is seeing the real," and that this is not done with the eyes, but through awareness. In this he was just as equipped to see what is truly important, the invisible truth, as anyone else. Whenever he was so oriented, he not only found himself peaceful and loving, but also noticed a sort of "sixth sense" by which he could navigate without awkwardness or mishap. But occasionally he was troubled by ambitions to be admired as competent, and to appear not blind, to seem to see. We named this person Victor the Visible. Whenever he was Victor the Visible, he walked into walls and fell up stairs. Even his guide dog became disoriented.

Side Effects of False Prayer

A man attending a conference developed a head cold that caused him to keep blowing his nose during meetings. He was embarrassed by the attention he felt this drew to himself, confiding later that he had "so hoped no one would notice me." But, upon further examination, he uncovered a secret ambition to be a conference leader himself. He was just waiting enviously until he would know enough to do this. His noisy, nosey head cold was a manifestation of this frustrated secret desire. He was just tooting his own horn, blowing his "knows," and drowning out everyone else's.

This man was suffering the side effects of connecting prayer. He thought constantly of getting others to confirm his ability to think and know. But since it is only Fundamental Mind/God that truly thinks and knows, he suffered sickening side effects of frustration and of never being inspired with Fundamental Mind's ideas. Having already recognized the unpleasant social side effects of behaving along these lines (talking too much, being argumentative, babbling, and so on), at the conference he was determined to stifle himself. When they were not allowed behavioral expression, his thoughts took somatic form.

As long as we engage in false connecting prayer, we continue to suffer side effects that are really nothing more than the false proving itself false. If we believe we have been truly praying, we complain that our prayers "didn't work." Some people claim that they never pray, because prayer is ineffective. Some who admit to praying explain "unanswered prayer" by saying that God, in his great mysterious wisdom, said "No." But all prayer (intentional or inadvertent) is effective to some extent in the sense that the thoughts always become manifest in some form. Is false, connecting prayer effective? Alas, yes. It can be a bad effect; as the above story shows, in experiential terms there is definitely a side effect. For example, one woman told me the following story:

I received a telephone call from a woman with whom I am serving on a committee. While we were speaking, my husband entered and began swearing about a mistake the bank had made. I didn't know what to do. I kept trying to soothe my husband and to pay attention to what the woman on the phone was saying. But pretty soon I was so distracted that I just became incoherent!

Distract means *pull from.* She was doubly distracted—pulled in two directions at once. But by what? Only her connecting prayers. She had a strong mental attachment to what the caller would think of her as a committee member. She had a strong mental attachment to what her husband thought of her as a wife. So the two conflicting demands for her attention were really only her own two demands for attention pulling her in two directions. She is like a fisherman who has caught two fish and is trying to get them both into the boat. She could have ignored her husband's outburst and finished her conversation, or excused herself from the call, or firmly asked her husband to wait. Perhaps he would not have thought to have a tantrum in front of her in the first place. But while she was so busy trying to haul in two people at once, no such intelligent ideas were occurring to her. Good ideas were available to her, but she was not available to them.

This shows the troublesomeness of false, connecting prayer. If she did not believe in God, her prayers probably ran something like, "How can I persuade my husband that I am an understanding wife while at the same time convince this woman that I am really 'together' and hide from her the fact that I married a raving maniac?" If she believed in God, her prayer was probably the same except for the addition of such phrases as, "Oh, God, please make her think. . . . Oh, God, please make him stop. . . . " Either way, it was her prayer that determined her experience, because it was only by the thought strings of her prayer that the situation was able to take place at all.

Once we have recognized our false connecting prayers, we are no longer so surprised that peace, harmony, and inspiration are not forthcoming. We are pulled by our own pullers. If we find ourselves in a tug of war, roped into something, hanging by a thread, at loose ends, tied down, strung along, or torn by tangled relationships, we have only our false connecting prayers to blame. Nothing is pulling on us that we did not mentally connect to or are not mentally attached to in the first place. No one has power over us whom we were not seeking mental power over to begin with. Our main problem in life is our connecting prayers. The primary misperception at the bottom of all these prayers is *I know*. The primary thing that has to be given up is our knowing what is good for us.

While the idea of God as mind may strike us as a comforting hypothesis, the idea that we might not have minds of our own seems terrifying. That we cannot and need not take thought for ourselves is inconceivable unless we realize the presence of Fundamental Mind. We dare not trust Fundamental Mind until we have proven its presence. We cannot prove its presence without relying on it. It is to help with this predicament that we turn at last to true spiritual prayer.

12. At Prayer and Aware: Dynamics of True Prayer

Trust in the Lord with all thine heart, and lean not unto thine own understanding; in all thy ways acknowledge him, and he will direct thy paths.

PROVERBS 3:6

True prayer begins with the premise that there is a mind beyond what is in our heads. Although we are not that mind, we are part of it; although we are not thinkers and knowers, we can participate in Fundamental Mind's ideas, and so be wisely and wonderfully provided for in life. The way in which we are part of Fundamental Mind is as consciousnesses.

When we thought we had to grow up and live "by our own wits," we were in effect *de-mented*. Inspiration was blocked by worry and calculation. Through spiritual prayer we are reminded and brought back into our right mind by seeing ourselves as part of, rather than apart from, Fundamental Mind, thereby opening ourselves to inspiration. This is *spiritual* prayer because it is focused on seeing rather than on dictating, doing, or getting. In spiritual prayer we realize that we not only cannot think and know *what will happen to me, what to do, who to count on, and how to get them to cooperate, or keep them from being taken from us*, but also that we need not do this because of the existence of Fundamental Mind, the One that keepeth us and "shall neither slumber nor sleep."[1]

Breaking the Mutual Hold

We cannot engage in true and false prayer simultaneously. We cannot simultaneously think and be aware. For spiritual prayer to occur, the mutual hold of thinker and thought must first be broken. It is a lot like floating. You cannot float until you know the water will hold you up; you cannot know this until you let go of everything else. More simply, we need to do two things that are the same: (1) to rely only on Fundamental Mind and (2) not to rely on anything else; just as the compass needle must (1) rely only on one point and (2) not bump into, rest on, or be attached to anything else.

In spiritual prayer we *let go of* what we mentally cling to in order to *let go into* Fundamental Mind. Only this way can we prove to ourselves that God is there. Letting go in order to float was hard, but it is nothing compared to the letting go required in prayer. In floating, we knew what we had to let go of. But in prayer, at first, we do not even know what we are hanging onto. The following steps can help: (1) separating the thinker from the thought; (2) recognizing the thought; (3) distinguishing between true and false thoughts; (4) resituating the situation; (5) resituating ourselves.

Separating Thinker from Thought

She was so glad to see her daughter when she came running out of school. "Hi, Darling," she said, as the child climbed into the car. "We'll just have time to stop at home before your skating lesson." She was not prepared for the darkness that now came over her daughter's face. "Oh, no! Not today!" groaned the girl. "I'm just not in the mood." Immediately the mother felt angry—really angry—inside.

Feelings come over us without our being aware of the thoughts behind them. Considering the importance of awareness, it is amazing how rarely we are aware of exactly what ideas we are entertaining. Whatever is in charge of consciousness is at that moment in charge of our lives. If false, then trouble. If true, harmony. We turn to prayer with the idea of letting Fundamental Mind determine the content of our consciousness and thereby guide our lives. We begin our prayer by distancing ourselves from our thoughts. We can discern, observe, consider, analyze, notice, behold, understand, contemplate, recognize thoughts, but we are not and do not generate our thoughts. It is not our job to decide or determine, only to "let that mind be in you which was also in Christ Jesus." We start by recognizing that the thinker is only an entertainer of thoughts, and that the thoughts we are entertaining are questionable.

"Wait a minute," the mother said to herself. "If I am disturbed, it is by my thoughts about what is happening. Before I say anything, I'd better take a little time to tune in. I need to see what thoughts are making me so upset." So instead of expressing her anger at her daughter, she kept still and waited to see what her own thoughts were.

Recognizing the Thought

By the time she got home, the mother's thoughts were clear and running rampant. "Here I go out of my way to pick up my daughter from school and take her to skating lessons, and she isn't a bit grateful. Oooh, she is so spoiled. What's the use of going to all this trouble and expense when she doesn't appreciate a thing that I'm doing for her?"

To receive Fundamental Mind's ideas, we first have to free ourselves from all thoughts that could not have come from Fundamental Mind. So the next step is to identify what is already "on our minds." To understand this, hold a finger close to your eye. If you look past it, you cannot see it well enough to identify it. There is a slight blurriness, but you cannot really see what is being blocked, let alone what is in the way. If it had always been there, you might not even notice the blurriness. Even if you did, you would either think it was the way you are, or "just a fact of life." But if you withdraw the finger a few inches, you see it is neither the way you are nor the nature of reality—it's only a finger. At this distance you see that you also have the choice of moving it out of the way. Everything is clear. There is nothing blurry about either your vision or the view. You are free and clear.

So it is with certain thoughts, especially those that entered consciousness when we were young and that we regard as reality, not as questionable thoughts. All are thoughts about what we want and believe we need. Most are mistaken ideas about ourselves in relation to others. Merely to recognize and disown those thoughts that have interpersonal conditions (*If they will, then I can . . . if they don't, then I can't . . . if I, then maybe they*) is already liberating. Whatever these thoughts are, once we see them as thoughts, the struggle of living around them already dies down somewhat. Before they were me; now they are mine, and I have the choice of paying attention to them *or to something else*. To reach this "point choice" is very important, because it is the point at which we begin to be able to let Fundamental Mind take charge of our lives. It is at this point that we really begin to have a choice at all. The Bible says, "Choose ye this day, whom ye shall serve."[2] Or we could say that we need to and now can choose this day, whom we shall serve, which idea of who we are (*self in relation to other* or *I and my Father are one*).

Behind every experience are certain thoughts that are mostly beliefs about who and what we need to connect up to in order to survive. Because many of these thoughts are from childhood, we are so identified with them that it is not easy to be objective about them. A good way to penetrate the haze is to ask not *what* but *who* was I thinking about. You may catch glimpses of people's faces. After that your thoughts may come into focus much as a dream is sometimes recalled. What was happening? What was I saying? With practice most find that their consciousness is a veritable Cecil B. DeMille movie set, crowded with actors and production assistants. One individual observed, "I am still not clear what my thoughts are, but I do see that I am always the star."

Dreams, fantasies, and experiences are all side effects that provide clues to our underlying thoughts. We hope eventually to learn to catch these thoughts as thoughts before they become manifest in experience, but early on it is mostly our experiences that drive us to prayer and bring our thoughts to our attention. Psychiatry helps us with this. Psychiatrist Thomas Hora, in particular, offers us the possibility of looking at fantasies, dreams, and experiences with the question, "What is the meaning of what seems to be?"[3] It would be hard to overrate this contribution that helps us discover the "mental equivalent" of our experience. It is a way of discovering what thoughts are running (and perhaps ruining) our lives.

Now the mother began to consider the thoughts behind her experience. "If I feel let down by my daughter, then there must be some way in which I am looking to her to hold me up. I started out by thinking that she depends on me for her good (the skating lessons, transportation, money, self-sacrifice), but evidently I am depending on her (for appreciation, acknowledgment of my goodness, enthusiasm). But why shouldn't I? Don't I have the right? Doesn't she owe me something?

A helpful pre-question is, "What seems to be?" Whether considering a fantasy, dream, or actual event, it helps to first describe it almost as if it were a painting, without looking for causes or solutions. Looking at a situation as a painting separates us from both the experience and the thought it expresses. Now we can ask, "What is the meaning of what seems to be?" or "What idea of self and life does this picture portray?"

During a counseling session, a man was repeatedly overcome with tears. Asked about the meaning of his crying, he said, "I am crying because I am so sad, because my mother, she . . . my father, he . . . my friends, they . . . and my bank account, it . . ." But those were not meanings. The question to consider was what was the meaning of his crying *in the session*. He realized that he rarely cried by himself, and then only while thinking of someone watching him do so. It became clear that the meaning of the tears was to get the counselor to pity him. He wanted to influence the counselor to feel sorry for him. To this end he wanted to look pitiful. What a goal! So certain questionable thoughts were discerned behind the picture. The uncontrollable crying suddenly ceased. He saw that there may be a better idea around which to conduct his life.

No one grows up without such mistaken ideas. We try to change or hide bad ones, to build on good ones. What we don't do is question them—even though some of them are pretty funny. For example, I knew an eighty-seven-year-old lady who was writing a book. It was wonderful because she had so much vitality, and as she went along her manuscript was becoming quite good. But the better it became, the more anxious she grew. She grew so miserable that once I suggested that she didn't have to write this book, especially if it were going to make her sick and upset. "Oh, no!" she cried. "It's very important for me to write it because my father would be so proud of me!" She was still trying to impress her father, even though he had already been dead for over forty years!

I knew another man who had been a Presbyterian all his life. But when he got to college he looked around and thought he might attend the Episcopal church for a change. The next time he went home he mentioned this to his mother. "Oh, no!" she cried. "That would kill your grandmother." Now the grandmother was already long dead, but nevertheless he remained a Presbyterian all his life. Some funny ideas are handed down for generations.

Facing the thoughts behind experiences, fantasies, and dreams is an important part of our prayer, and it is the longest part of any counseling work. It is fairly easy to teach receptive spiritual students the logic of the spiritual perspective. But it is quite another matter for people to rely on and let these ideas actually take hold, heal, and reshape their lives. The timing of the rising to the surface of the deepest hidden, hurtful thoughts around which each individual's protective ways are formed is a matter of mystery and grace. But by the time they do rise and can be recognized they are as frail as bubbles floating away. Only what is finally admissible becomes dismissible. When and whether to seek counseling, with whom, is also a matter of mysterious grace. If it is good for you, when you are ready, you will know—and whatever you are ready for is what will be available. But along with and forever after any counseling work, the private prayerful confronting of the thoughts behind our experiences and fantasies is pivotal to all healing and transcendence.

Distinguishing Between True and False Thoughts

When they reached home, the daughter was still pouting and the mother was still raging inside. Wisely, the mother continued to keep still. She poured her daughter a glass of milk to go with the cookies that were on the table. Then, looking out the window, she began to examine her own thoughts for their validity in the light of spiritual truth.

The value of having discovered our thoughts is that we can then evaluate them. This way we can free ourselves from the terrible hold of false ones and make way for better ones to take charge. There are two kinds of thoughts: false and true. Just knowing this much can already be helpful. One woman suffered constant rejection. She always tried to be nice, never raised her voice, and went out of her way to do things for others. Yet no one returned her kindness, and time and again she found herself abandoned, even shunned by those to whom she had been so nice. In one of our first counseling sessions, she realized that being nice can be a way of using people. "What a relief!" she exclaimed. "I thought it was *me*, but now I see that my idea of being nice is not so nice! No wonder! Whew! What a relief!" She saw that we can only be abused by those we wish to use, and she began to explore what it means to be in love together as an alternative to trying to get love from each other.

That night she dreamed of a little girl in her house who had AIDS. The child was crying because she knew she was going to be thrown out of the house, rejected because of her sickness. But in the dream the woman went to the child and took her in her arms, and held her close. "No, no," she said. "It's all right. You are all right, and you may stay right here with me." For so long she had thought there was something intrinsically unlovable about her. But when she discovered that the problem was only a mistaken idea, she was finally able to know that she was all right and thus to accept herself. This was the beginning of a lessening of her drive to seek acceptance, which was the beginning of her letting love take place in her life.

How wonderful to recognize the presence of a mistaken idea as a mistaken idea! Such notions have power only if they are believed in and only as long as the belief lasts. Even before truth is realized, guilt, blame, and bitterness begin to die, and inspired ideas get born as we begin to see what questionable ideas we are living around.

How can we tell true thoughts from false? Every true idea comes from and can be traced back to Fundamental Mind. Anything that can't be traced to one underlying mind has no basis in reality and is no basis for living. You can trace your thoughts by mentally drawing lines. Our earlier story of the distracted woman on the telephone illustrates this. If you drew lines to trace her thought, you would see that she has a line going out to her husband and a line to the caller and a line coming back from her husband and a line coming back from the caller. Through these lines she is trying to get them both to think of and react to her in certain ways.

Most of our thoughts run between self and other and do not trace back to or emanate from God. Any thought in which the good of one individual is regarded as dependent on another does not trace back to God, but that is how we think—fishing, tugging, yanking, hog-tying, and even whipping each other with the thought tentacles of our connecting prayers. Do unto others in such a way that they will do for you.

Though it seems reasonable not to want to be a stupid, ugly, weak, un-nice, outcast loser, the inevitable extension of these interpersonal lines of reasoning (in other words, to want to be a smart, gorgeous, strong, virtuous, admired winner) is neither reasonable nor nice. If you believe that to be loved you have to prove to others that you are nice and right, you will also wind up trying to prove that you are nicer or righter *than* others. This is a losing battle, because of course they will never love you for making them feel less bright and good. How long the fighting! How brief and bittersweet the victories! We may think boxing is brutal and grueling, yet no matter how many brutal rounds a boxing match lasts, it is nothing compared to our lifelong conquests of each other. The pleasurable resulting ego orgasms are so pitifully brief. *My, my aren't we grown up? How smart, how strong, how right, how good you are!* Ahhhhh! So much struggle for such feeble little explosions of self.

How can we trace everything back to God? By reviewing everything from the premise that God is, that there is only one Fundamental Mind, and that it is the only power source. Whenever we enter a new situation, it is good to pray in this way.

For example, when you think of a telephone conversation, you tend to visualize two people connected by one string. The lines of communication are regarded as interpersonal. Often it is not communication that is the issue at all, but rather the "putting across" of oneself. So some feel that they don't "do well" on the phone and are afraid to make calls, while others would much prefer to call than to meet face to face. This is hilariously portrayed by a character in Neil Simon's play *Come Blow Your Horn*. Every time the telephone rings, the sixty-ish woman runs to answer it. No matter how many times it has rung by the time she gets there, she always stops to smooth out her lap wrinkles, tug at her suit jacket, and put her hair into place before picking up the receiver. The mounting guffaws of the audience at each repetition of this ludicrous ritual reveal what a common chord it strikes. Even before she knows who the caller is or what the call is about, she is concerned about how she will "come across" to the caller. She regards the phone conversation as a situation in which she may or may not succeed in "putting herself across" and winning the caller's admiration and support.

However, even as you go to the phone, you can pray from a truer perspective. Recognize that the parent/child person-to-person perspective is erroneous. Acknowledge that there is only one mind of which each of you is an aspect. As you lift the receiver let your question be not, *Who's there and what should I say?* but, *Hmm, I wonder what is about to be revealed? I wonder what needs to be understood? I wonder what God has in mind? Now what? Speak Lord, for thy servant heareth.*[4]

In the first way, the lines are drawn between two minds. In the second way, all lines run back to God. The first is a tug-of-war in the making. In the second there is listening, regard, receptivity—a clear runway on which clarity and love can come in for a landing. Sometimes I "preprayer" in this way; sometimes I don't. It is easy to guess in which calls there is more communication, harmony, understanding, even healing and love taking place. Reorienting in such small, daily situations is a helpful way to cultivate the practice of prayerful living and to study the difference between God-reliant and person-reliant perspectives.

One woman complained of never having had a childhood because her parents were too disturbed to take care of her. At fifty, she still thought of herself as a motherless child. In counseling she was told that, in reality, "God is and has always been your mother." Now, aged and ailing, her parents required constant care which, ironically, fell entirely on her shoulders. Desperate to get free, the daughter sought help.

It was suggested that she look for her stake in the situation, that is, for anything in the circumstance that she might be reluctant to let go of. She could see that she regarded her life as a motherless child as heroic. She was Little Orphan Annie. In a way she was addicted to being a heroine—a heroine addict—whom in fantasy everyone, including her parents, would therefore finally love. Being her parents' parent was the ultimate heroism of the motherless child. As much as she resented the script—her lack of freedom, the thankless work—she was nevertheless secretly unwilling to give up her part in the melodrama. She still saw herself as a motherless child whose mother should mother her; but she had made quite a life as the Child Who Had to Take Care of Her Own Mother. By caring for her parents, she was living off them—just as if they had been taking care of her. You could just see it on the marquee! The common thought connection between this mother and daughter was, *You take care of me (tug), no, YOU take care of ME!* Only if at least one would let go and trace her life back to God could either be freed from their tug-of-war. But recognizing the issue was an important, liberating step.

Looking out the window, the mother traced the lines of her thought and saw that there was no God in them. They ran back and forth between herself and her daughter. They said she was the source of her daughter's good, and in return the daughter should be the source of hers. She gave up certain things (time, money, pleasure, accomplishment) for the daughter, the daughter should give up something for her (be happy, be grateful, appreciate the mother, be in the mood, love the lessons). Somehow, for her to be happy, the daughter had to give up what she wanted; and, for the daughter to be happy, the mother had to give up what she wanted. Only one of them could be happy at a time. Was this an idea that God could have? No.

Resituating the Situation

When we trace our lives back to God, we are replacing false thoughts with true, thereby reviewing or resituating our entire situation in reality. We no longer look at life as happening entirely between each other ("Off them I live and move and get my being"), but in Fundamental Mind ("In God we live and move and have our being. I and my Parent are one"). This can happen through deliberate acknowledgment or through spontaneous inspiration. More and more as we practice spiritual prayer, once a false idea has been questioned, fresh inspiration comes. It just bubbles up and takes over when we even consider reviewing our situation with reference to Fundamental Mind. The rest is easy because we don't have to do it.

I once had an office that faced the Hudson River. Sometimes students would complain, "It's so hard. I can't do it. When will I ever see it?" So then I would ask, "How would you go about seeing the Hudson River from here?" That was easy. Everyone understood that all you had to do was look out the window that faced the river. And how do you form the picture of the Hudson river? Shores, trees, sky, palisades, boats? That was clear, too. The answer is that you don't have to form the picture. Once you are looking in the right direction, the river does all the rest of the work. You don't have to think the river or do the picture, only to pay attention.

The same is true with the presence and guidance of God. We have to pay attention, but then Fundamental Mind does the rest of the work. You can just get still and see what God has in mind for you at any given moment. Now you are the riverbed for the flow of divine ideas. Now this stream is flowing through you, remolding and reshaping your life. When I was first learning to pray, I was very ambitious about enlightenment. I wanted to get it. I tried to do it. It was self-centered and "unsuccessful." One day, while attempting to meditate, a Bible passage came to mind: "Know ye that the Lord he is God; it is he that hath made us and not we ourselves."⁵ Since I already knew the words, I wondered whether it was really inspiration or whether I was just "thinking" it myself—from memory.

Suddenly it occurred to me that if there was only one mind I couldn't think anything by myself. If any good ideas were coming, they must be from God! I was so struck that for a moment I was still. Quietly four words crept into consciousness—all adverbs describing ways of being: *slowly, surely, simply, purely.* It wasn't necessary to be ambitious about getting to God—only to conduct my daily life in a Godly way. *It is he that hath made us and not we ourselves.* I did not have to get to God; God would get to me. If I would allow it. Slowly. Surely. Simply. Purely. There couldn't have been a better idea for me at that moment.

This fact that inspiration comes is one of our first proofs of God as mind. Sometimes it comes without our asking: a little message to double check something, the sudden dissolution of a problem. Notice these moments. They are when God speaks. Go with the thought that God has brought to mind. Go where it tells you, and go to God. Tracing the idea to Fundamental Mind, you discover God. Recognize that this idea came when you needed it. Notice that you did not think of it, it dawned on you. "You shall hear a voice behind you saying, This is the way, walk ye in it."⁶

Did you hear it once? That means it is there! There for the listening and trusting. Behind, before, beside, beneath, below, beyond. From beyond everything that seems to be, the voice of God is heard by those who listen. This is frequently brought home to me on Wednesdays. Every Wednesday I conduct two spiritual growth seminars—one in the morning, one at night, in two different towns, in two different states, with two entirely different groups of people. I never plan an agenda for these meetings, but rather wait for a member of the group to bring up a question or concern. More often than not the question raised by the first speaker in each meeting will be the same. More often than not, as the meeting progresses, several others will exclaim, "This is just what I wanted to ask about today!" Many times it happens that as I am preparing for the day, an idea will come rather strongly to my attention so that I think to myself, *I wonder if this will turn out to be the topic of today's session?* Often it is! As Isaiah says of God, "Before they call, I answer."[7]

I knew a woman who studied a spiritual teaching for many years, but was plagued all the time by doubts about whether God really existed. One day she told me a story and asked a question:

Recently my children have been studying a caterpillar, which they were keeping in a jar in the kitchen. According to a book we have, it is important to keep some water in the jar for humidity. But yesterday, as I passed by, the thought crossed my mind that we needed to revise the setup, because it was possible that the caterpillar could fall into the water and drown. I had the thought, but I did not stop to do anything about it. Later, when I was finished with everything else I wanted to do, I came back into the kitchen and found that the caterpillar had drowned. I felt terrible and guilty about the caterpillar, but then I also thought about the fact that I had received in time the needed idea that would have saved the caterpillar, if I had listened to it. I think maybe that idea came from God? Do you?

I was very happy for this individual, because finally she had had a firsthand glimpse that there is a source beyond self and other of precise and timely guidance for her life. I reassured her that the caterpillar had not died in vain.

From out of the blue, Fundamental Mind's ideas may arise within us as inspiration, or through someone else. They may take the form of circumstance, companion, opportunity, request, invitation, or a peaceful, loving state of mind. This providence never ceases. It is only a question of whether or not we recognize it.

One week I saw two students who misunderstood this. An unexpected call prevented one from missing an airplane. An incidental conversation saved one from purchasing inappropriate, unnecessary equipment for her office, a move that would have made her worst fears of incompetency in her new job come true. Instead of being happy, both were depressed. "Why didn't I think of that?" they said. "Why do others think of such things, and I don't? What's the matter with me that I am not smarter and more independent?" It was so silly, because of course the wonderful thing was that the needed idea had arrived at the necessary time without anyone engineering or "knowing" anything. One just "happened to call," the other "to drop by." There was everything to be grateful for, because it was a beautiful demonstration of participation in Fundamental Mind.

Sometimes when people feel helpless enough about something to think of God, they ask, "How can I bring God into this situation?" This is backwards. First of all, the situation is a manifestation of our belief that we live in a realm other than God, a world of mind-in-body among other minds-in-bodies. God is left completely out. But if we try to bring God into this situation, we are regarding God as just another person at our disposal. We can't leave God out of the situation, but we can't bring God into the situation either. Instead we can prayerfully *bring the situation into God* by tracing everything back to Fundamental Mind and subtracting everything that doesn't. When we prayerfully resituate the situation this way, many difficulties simply dissolve, things begin to fall into place, and intelligent responses to life become clear.

"No," realized the mother, "God could not have an idea that my good would depend on my daughter's bad or that my daughter's good would depend on my bad. God does not say, 'Off each other they live and move and get their being.' God is being good in every direction at once. Therefore, each moment of my life as it is presented to me is a present of the

good of God for me at that moment. If I don't see the good of God in this moment of my life, then I am just tossing this gift away unwrapped." She looked around at her daughter, who was sitting peacefully at the kitchen table, patting the dog and resting her head on her hand. How dear she was! How beautiful she had looked running toward the car! How happy the mother had been when it had been time to put aside her paperwork to go and pick up her daughter! What a nice change of pace! What a privilege! What a rich, full life! Moment by moment.*

Consider this picture of several sticks on end: / / / /. If we regard ourselves in this stick way, as separate minds in bodies, it seems necessary to lean against each other to keep from falling over, getting knocked down, or sinking away altogether. Falling every which way, we grab at each other, trying to depend, defend, and strike a balance. Everything is full of conflict and insecurity. But if we remove the frame and step back, we find an entirely different picture: ᘈᘈᘈ. After all, each stick was not a precarious separate thing, but the tip of a wave, upheld, supplied, and organized in relation to all other waves by the deep ocean beneath.

In this situation the idea that one wave has to depend on another for supply or support is absurd. Likewise, when we can see beyond self and other, we become aware of the unseen spiritual force beneath us that not only holds us up but is in fact swelling up as us. It gives us our security, our being. It organizes us in loving relation to each other, and takes shape as everything needed and more. Once we see everyone and everything as an aspect of Fundamental Mind, instead of minds-in-bodies battling for life, we discover one mind emanating in all directions. In this resituated situation love is possible at last.

Resituating Ourselves

So far we have been talking about contemplative prayer, a quiet matter of paying attention, discerning, listening. True prayer can be contemplative or existential. In contemplative prayer we receive inspiration from Fundamental Mind. In existential or living prayer, we obey that inspiration *with all our heart and with all our mind and with all our strength,* in thought, word, and deed, and way of being. It is often not until we commit ourselves in living prayer that the truth and reliability of what comes to us in contemplative prayer becomes a firsthand realization.

Both kinds of prayer are necessary, and one flows naturally into the other. Even after we glimpse the truth in contemplative prayer, our prayer is not complete. We still have to take the plunge, and actually trust our lives to Fundamental Mind rather than to our own fearful thought takings. Contemplative prayer re-minds us of the possibility of switching from the connection-making to a oneness-seeing perspective and helps us make the switch. But we also need to pray existentially, "easing ourselves into the boundless just where it touches us" by (1) trusting in Fundamental Mind, and (2) not in anything else.

Since most problems are by-products of erroneous survival-seeking thoughts, it is very hard to give them up. We dare not give them up for good until we see that they are not necessary. The secret is to give them up just for a moment. Just for one moment I will not mentally reach out for support from anything. Until then (no matter how much we understand in principle) we are like nonswimmers who believe floating is possible. We may memorize the entire swimming manual, even explain it to others, but we are still sitting on our beach towel. We are saying, "Yes, yes, I see. We can swim! Isn't it wonderful?" But we aren't floating because we haven't even gotten wet yet! Our prayer is not finished until we have jumped in and staked our lives on whatever is coming in prayer. This is existential or living prayer. It must be what James meant by, "Be ye doers of the word, and not hearers only."[8] Not doing exactly, but putting your life on the line. It is absolutely necessary in order to verify that the mind of God is really there.

Whenever I have an opportunity to work with children and teenagers, I like to introduce them to this idea of prayer as the way they can find out for themselves whether God, as a higher source of guidance, exists: "When you're down, or stuck, or afraid," I tell them, "before you go to your parents or some other adult, and before you struggle very long on your own, try this: sit down, get still, remember God, and see if a good idea occurs to you that you didn't have a minute ago." Next time we meet, I ask if anybody tried it. I was very struck by one boy's account. "Yes," he said. "On Monday I had a terrible day at school. There were all kinds of things that I hadn't done that I should have. And I had done lots of things that I shouldn't have. I was feeling very angry at myself, real depressed. I went to my room in this horrible mood. Then I remembered our class and decided to try praying. So I sat up on my bed [he demonstrated how he had sat—erect and still, feet on the floor] and just waited. Right away this thought popped into my head: *Clean your room.* Well, even though I felt so bad, I began to clean my room, which was a huge mess. You know, I got really into it! Pretty soon I found all my old papers and report cards with all the nice things different teachers had said about me and my work. By the time I finished, I was feeling fine about myself. And my room was so nice that instead of going out I just stayed there and studied."

The next day the boy happened to stop by. "You know, there was one part that I forgot to mention in class," he said. "Ever since I cleaned my room, I have had this idea to start cleaning up our house." Now this was pretty impressive, because he lived alone with his father, who had been quite ill for a number of years. The house was always a mess, and the son had never been taught or been moved by others' suggestions to be very helpful, but here he had received both the idea and the motivation through his own prayer. It was lovely to see how he had first received the guidance to live more intelligently and how this had mushroomed into love—living love.

A few weeks later, the father finally died. The boy could look back on a time when he had helped his dad. It was lovely to see how he had become more aware of the presence of his heavenly Father's guidance just before the disappearance of his earthly father. At the funeral, he rose and spoke with inspiring assurance.

"There is one thing I know my father knew for sure," he began, "and that is where he came from . . .

"And I know that the most important thing for us all," he concluded at the end of his remarks, "is to remember where we come from, and where we are going."

It is amazing what the still small voice can accomplish, if we just sit still and listen to it.

The purpose of living prayer is to resign the post of mastermind, to begin living moment by moment. The idea is to lose our life to find it by losing our mind to find it. Instead of taking thought for what is supposed to happen later, how a problem is to be solved or a goal achieved, see whether there is enough guidance, meaning, purpose, fulfillment, support, for living this moment. For just this one moment, live by and rely on the sufficiency of the immediately available truth as if you *knew* it was reliable. Wishes and fears may not leave us entirely, but they can be momentarily set aside. That's when, not before, we feel this force beneath us. We cannot feel its force until we are relying on it utterly. For example, tune in now to the next episode of "The Heroine Addict."

The aged mother of the heroine addict was also addicted to being the heroine. Both loved to be martyrs, complaining competitively about the heroic hardship of being poorly taken care of by each other. One particularly troublesome problem was that, despite the persuasion of doctors, nurses, daughter, and husband, the old lady refused to use her walker. Without exercise, her ability to walk was deteriorating, her dependency increasing. One night the daughter realized that with the mother completely bedridden her parents would be unable to stay in their home and would have to come and live with her. Then she would have to take care of them twenty-four hours a day instead of only eight.

She was filled with such dread that she began to pray. "God is my mother. God is my mother's mother. I do not know what will happen tomorrow. I do not have to know what will happen tomorrow. I do not know how this problem will be solved. I do not have to know. God is my mother, and at this moment everything is all right." For a moment she set aside all her concerns.

Peace came, and she slept like a baby. In the morning, when she went to her parents' home, her mother met her at the door. She was using her walker to hike laps around the apartment! "It came to me in the night," the mother said, "that the worst thing that could happen would be to lose my freedom to walk."

While the daughter was busy seeking her own needed inspiration, the mother received directly from God the very idea she needed, which all the king's horses and all the king's men had not been able to force on her. So began a time of letting go that led eventually to the freedom of both mother and daughter from their longstanding suffering together.

The fact that God's ideas come whenever we look for them is evidence of the existence of the mind of God. The fact that harmony occurs when we *rely* on God's ideas is proof of God's goodness. It is through our reliance that seeing turns into being and intelligence becomes love. This is how we verify the presence of God as Fundamental Mind, which not only runs the universe but also, carefully and tenderly, personally mentors us.

Awareness that we live and move and have our being in God as mentor frees us from having to put out thought tentacles in all directions and releases us from all that entangles, tugs, and tears at us. After all, our connecting thoughts are all based on the idea, *I should not sink, therefore something should hold me up.* When we turn to spiritual prayer, we encounter the mind of God, the mentor that will uphold us if we allow it to do so. As there is something in the water that holds me up, so in all life the mentor is there to support and sustain me whenever I rely on it. It takes place within me as inspiration, vitality, and love; it takes place without as support, providence, guidance, companionship, opportunity, and love. Everything within and without comes from and manifests this mind of God. All things working together for good. In times of uncertainty I like to remind myself that *I can trust God as far as I can trust him,* by which I mean that when I trust Fundamental Mind (and not anything else) it becomes the upholding force in my life. God is as reliable as I am reliant.

Some things are beyond understanding, and we have to humbly accept that they are beyond our understanding. Once I sat with a man in terrible suffering. He had Alzheimer's and Parkinson's disease, and one of his legs had just been amputated. His whole predicament seemed to call the very idea of God into question. We were working together, trying to keep his mind off the pain that was mounting as the drugs wore off. While I talked and lit his cigarettes and, at his request, even tried to adjust his stump into a more comfortable position, I prayed. Trying not to know what either my right or left hand were doing I prayed. I prayed not only for him, but for myself—to see beyond this awfulness any truth, affirming that understanding is possible, that God's ideas from above can reach us anytime, that when they come, they draw us up not only out of trouble but to a higher place, that what was before me either could not really be or was not all that it seemed. Suddenly the man spoke. "You know," he said, "I am seeing the most amazing unfolding of love." He did not request another cigarette. The pain subsided before the next injection.

As the child slips her hand into her parent's, so we slip awareness into mind. It is not a matter of looking out for oneself or of depending on others to avoid annihilation in a mindless, malicious milieu. Fundamental Mind, God, is the whole milieu and everything in it! When we pray we discover our oneness with the Father, which is not a person holding our hand but the Fundamental Mindforce of the universe. Before Adam discovered his "self," everything was the perfect multifaceted expression of God, including Adam, his companion, food, employment. Had Adam seen the significance of it all, he would have discovered Fundamental Mind taking place everywhere—as providence, love, vitality, inspiration, everything needed, as needed.

A Cambodian child was asked how he managed after his parents, brothers, and sisters were killed, his home taken from him. At the age of eight he had no idea how to take care of himself, and all who had cared for him before were gone. "After I saw that there was no one left, I realized I had to leave the country," he said. He described how he had escaped through the jungle to Thailand. "How did you know where to go?" they asked. "I followed the monkey trails," he said. "How did you know what to eat?" "I ate what the monkeys ate. They threw food down to me." Now he is a smiling teenager living a new life with a new family in America. He is a survivor.

His story is not exceptional.[9] Too many other Asian children have had similar experiences. As you listen to these miracle children you hear the same things repeatedly. They had no other recourse and above all no thought that they were supposed to know. They just followed and were led along by one idea, one monkey, one falling banana after another.

If everyone understood what these children demonstrate, perhaps they would not have had to experience the horrors they experienced. So it is for these and future dear ones even more than for ourselves that we prayerfully seek what Adam overlooked and Jesus realized. In a process of endless awakening, we seek awareness of our undividedness from Fundamental Mind until we no longer cling in child/parent relationship to everything and everyone in sight, because we know that I and my Father are one.

Feeling much more peaceful, the mother realized that it wasn't that her daughter didn't appreciate the lessons. She loved skating, and it was a joy to watch her skate. It was only that she had forgotten today was the day. It had taken her by surprise. Who knew what had been on her child's mind when she came from her busy school day? The mother glanced at the clock. No, there was no need to disturb her daughter yet. They still had ten more minutes before it was really necessary to leave for skating. Now that she had remembered where her good came from, the mother sought to see what the good of this moment was. She didn't need to use her daughter. So what was the good, the use of this moment? What was God's use for her at this moment? It occurred to her that she just had time to clear up her desk, which she did. Suddenly the door to her office

flew open, and her daughter burst in. "Hi Mom," she said breathlessly.
"We'd better hurry. It's almost time to leave. I'll get my skates."

> O Lord, my heart is not lifted up;
> My eyes are not raised too high.
> I do not occupy myself with things
> too great and marvelous for me.
> But I have calmed and quieted my soul.
> Like a child that is quieted at its mother's breast.
> Oh, Israel, trust in the Lord.
> From this time forth and forever more.[10]

Release and ye shall be released.[11]

The Notion of Notions

One day a piece of sand slipped into a baby oyster's shell. Her parents said "Ugh! How filthy you are!" Ashamed, she quickly closed her shell. But now the sand pressed into her painfully. She covered it with a secretion called mother of pearl, which hardened into something smooth, round, shiny, and white. This hid the ugly sand and kept it from hurting. When her parents saw the pearl, they were very proud. "How clever you are!" The baby oyster felt very good, and began to work hard on her pearl. She polished, smoothed, and built on it. "You are truly a pearl of a girl," her parents sighed happily.

But, except to display the pearl, the oyster hardly ever opened her shell. Mostly she kept it closed to protect her pearl. She worked until the pearl was so big that there was hardly any room for the oyster. Though the pearl was beautiful, the oyster felt crowded and unhappy. She was weary from working. She felt lonely and trapped.

Finally she went to a wise seal, who advised her to give up her pearl. "I could never do that," the oyster cried. "It's my whole life!"

"No," said the seal, "it's your whole problem. You have mistaken this pearl for your life, but it is nothing but a worthless piece of sand. You have given your whole life to beautifying this grit of sand, but it is nothing but spit on grit. It does not belong to you, and you do not belong to it. You are an oyster, and you belong to the sea."

"But what *is* an oyster?" she cried.

"You will never find out," said the wise seal, "until you have given up your pearl."

At last the oyster opened her shell and let go. The sea washed away the pearl, and the oyster beheld the sea's vast beauty. "Oh," she sighed softly. "I see."

Our most troublesome thoughts are those about ourselves. They can be called *parent thoughts,* not only because they came from our parents but because we get our ideas about who we are from them. Whether we try to live up to these thoughts or to live them down, as long as we hold onto them, we continue to model ourselves after them, to be their children.

All false connecting prayers arise from a child/parent perspective on life. There is a certain substructure. There are parent thoughts of who we think we are and survival thoughts of how to survive as who we think we are. Parent thoughts are not easy to identify or face. Survival thoughts are easier to identify than to face. All parent and survival thoughts have one thing in common: connecting to others. Our motive is to get love from each other. We learned to walk for freedom, to talk for understanding. But our parents said, "How wonderful you are for walking. We love you for that." And we thought, *Oh? Walking and talking are for getting love?*

The biggest error that got slipped in here is that love is something we get from somebody—at first from our parents, but later from others. So we have learned to relate to the whole universe in a child/parent way, hiding what seem to be liabilities in the eyes of others, capitalizing on our assets, never finding out what we really are. General Patton's father wanted his son to be a tough, super-masculine guy. As a boy he accepted without question his father's standards as his own. So, in order to sustain his father's love, Patton spent hours before a mirror trying to hide the sweetness in his face, learning to scowl and look tough.

To us the world is full of surrogate parents from whom we seek so-called love in order to get sustenance, to sustain ourselves. No idea is so troublesome as this one that we are to get love *from each other,* and that this is a matter of life and death. This is the notion of all notions. As long as we have such a parent/child relationship to the universe, we will also have sibling rivalry with everyone in it. It can't work. Like all travesties, this travesty of love deteriorates into tragedy, as is powerfully symbolized in the Bible by the fact that Adam and Eve's children, Cain and Abel, are out to kill each other.

Jesus said, "In this world ye shall have tribulation, but be of good cheer; I have overcome the world."[12] The I that overcomes the world of hate, hurt, fear, and frustration is the I of "I and my Parent are one." The shift from false connecting prayer to true spiritual prayer is from a child/parent perspective to I and my Parent are one. In true prayer we cease being the child of child/parent thoughts from the past and become the child of Fundamental Mind in the present. Here we are born again every moment, continually reborn—"pure and fresh and sinless in thy holy eyes." Life and us in it. Us and everything in our lives.

These are just some of the dynamics of spiritual prayer. Each prayer needs to include this progression of separating ourselves from our thoughts, recognizing the thoughts, distinguishing between the false and true, resituating the situation; and, in existential prayer, consciously resituating ourselves and obeying new ideas fresh from God. They are not just stages of prayer, but of life.

Eventually our whole life becomes a living prayer, a wonderful endless awakening. We cannot expect transformation from just knowing the stages of prayer, but they are road maps that can help us approach life prayerfully. Henceforth—desire by desire, fear by fear, situation by situation, and now by now—we pray to see our way through dark appearance to the invisible light. It cannot be accomplished in one book. It is a wonderful, lifelong journey and our entire reason for being.

13. The Practice of Prayer

When Gautama, at the end of his life, bid his followers to be "islands" to themselves, he meant that they should be islands in this ocean of universal Mindfulness, washed by Its encircling waters, filled with the sound of Its rhythmic voice, anchored in the plumbless depths of Its peace. To become such an island is the purpose of all Buddhist meditation.

It is equally, of course, the purpose of the Christian practice of mental prayer or of the Taoist practice of the "Circulation of the Light and Protection of the Centre," of which it is written that "when one begins to apply this magic, it is as if, in the middle of one's being, there were a non-being. When in the course of time the work is finished, and beyond the body there is another body, it is as if, in the middle of the non-being, there were a being."

There is nothing fanciful about this experience. It happens exactly as it is described here, as those who have persisted in true meditation can testify. The transference of will and attention from a false centre to a true one, from the eccentric to the concentric, is magical or, as a Chrisitian would say, a gift of Grace, in so far as it is, like all creative acts, not our own doing. But it is also the unfailing consequence of recognizing certain laws and learning to conform to them.

HUGH L'ANSON FAUSSET

According to the Bible, we have to be born again, "not of blood, nor of the will of the flesh, nor of the will of man, but of God. . . . Except a man be born again, he cannot see the kingdom of God. . . . Except a man be born of water and of the Spirit he cannot enter the kingdom."[1] The rebirth spoken of is perceptual, a matter of becoming aware of the true source and substance of our being. It means coming to see our lives not as products of others, neither of self-determination, but from the perspective of oneness with God. Prayer is our way of coming to this awareness, which can only be spiritually discerned.

It is said that we become "as little children" in rebirth. The essential difference between children and adults is their approach to life. The child approaches experience as an opportunity for understanding; the grown-up regards understanding as the means of determining experience. The child is primarily a learning, seeing creature who floats from one experience to the next in joyful anticipation of seeing what's new. The grown-up is primarily a calculating creature who moves through transitions only strenuously, trying to manage experience by means of elaborate stratagems. Children allow life to master them; adults struggle to master life.

When we are born again as children of God, we return to our early love of discovery wherein we find joy not in experience as such but in endless awakening. So the reborn child of God, like the very young child, is primarily a see-er, a seeing being. The more we realize what it means to be a child of God the more we are interested in prayer. Eventually prayer grows from something we take time out for occasionally and becomes our way of being. But in the beginning practice is required. There is no end to what can be written about prayer and prayerful living, but here are a few guidelines that may be helpful.

How Much and How Often?

The question often arises as to how much time to devote to prayer. Some say they don't have time for prayer. Their children won't leave them alone or they have to make a train or they're in a busy time right now and when they get their taxes in, *then* they will have time for prayer. They want to know how to deal with this problem of not having enough time.

To start the day or go from any situation to another without prayerfully acknowledging one's reliance on Fundamental Mind is like trying to drive your car without starting it. If you have a hole in the floor and very strong legs, maybe you can walk your car around like a kiddie car and make it look as if it is really running. But you won't get anywhere, except to the hospital with a hernia. Fundamental Mind is the only power. Prayer is the key for letting this power run our lives. When you understand this, you will never set foot out the door without prayer anymore than you would say, "It's too late to look for my car keys. I'll just have to go without them," and then dash out the door, jump into the car, and expect it to go.

Almost more than the praying itself, choosing to pray is so important. Choosing a moment of contemplative prayer is itself living prayer. It is putting one's life on the line and fulfilling the first commandment by putting God first. This doesn't have to take long. A simple acknowledgment can do—if it's genuine. But prayer does have to come first.

"Preprayeration"

On the other hand, even to remember that this choice of prayerfully opening oneself to Fundamental Mind exists, it is necessary to build up our consciousness. So it is also good to set aside regular times for study and prayer, say half an hour three times a day. One of these needs to be the first thing in the day, one the very last. It is not that prayer takes so long, or even that more time is better. But if Fundamental Mind is at the bottom of things, then we need to give it top priority. Viewpoint precedes understanding, which precedes mode of being, which precedes what takes place.

If you want to be an Olympic champion, you build your body by nourishing it regularly and substantially. We are building consciousness. We have only just discovered how crucial consciousness is in determining the running of our lives. Now, still, as life rises up around us in the form of events and circumstances, we forget that consciousness is key. We need at least three spiritual meals a day just to build up our awareness of awareness. This way we increase our understanding of what's what and what isn't so and begin to let *what is* take charge. Do anything necessary—lock yourself in the bathroom, stay in the car for a moment when you come home—to avail yourself of three square spiritual meals a day.

One woman reported that after a few days of being a bit cranky, her husband asked her what was the matter.

"Oh," she sighed, "I guess I just haven't been having my three spiritual meals a day."

"Well," he said, "next time you'd better have a double helping."

Some assume that if a little study and prayer is good, more will be better. This is not necessarily so. Sometimes people get into a frenzy about making others leave them alone for meditation. They put the lives of their entire family on hold, and nothing is getting done, and everyone is being tyrannized by their so-called prayer times. But it is quality not quantity that counts. Spiritual gluttony isn't the answer. If you eat three healthy meals a day and exercise in between, you develop a healthy body; if you eat all day you just get fat. If you take time for spiritual nourishment (contemplative prayer), you will develop spiritual awareness, but if you study and meditate without exercise (living prayer), you are just becoming a fathead.

The Secret Place

And when thou prayest, thou shalt not be as the hypocrites are: for they love to pray standing in the synagogues and in the corners of the streets, that they may be seen of men. Verily I say unto you, They have their reward. But thou, when thou prayest, enter into thy closet, and when thou hast shut thy door, pray to thy Father which is in secret: and thy Father which seeth in secret shall reward thee openly.[2]

Secrecy is another important element in the practice of prayer. It is much easier to be still and focused when we are not surrounded by others, especially since the main task in prayer is to shift from reliance on others to reliance on Fundamental Mind. The childish ego will appropriate any means of getting attention from others—even prayer. We hope, for example, that others will notice how deep, holy, or sensitive we are. So even though our prayer may be filled with truthful formulations, we may still be praying in the false connecting way. By praying in secret, we protect ourselves from fooling ourselves that we are praying while really we are not.

Some say, "I can never find a quiet place, my house is full of people, and there is no place where I can be alone." But it is just a matter of interest—and the willingness to be alone. When my children were very young and we lived in a small apartment, I discovered that the bathroom was one place where even they did not think of barging in. Since then, I have more than once taken advantage of this universal place of sanctuary, ducking in to restore perspective when I could not be still enough in the presence of others.

Even if we do not need to go off by ourselves to pray, we need to pray often. As the body consumes food and sorts out the waste, so consciousness is constantly taking in thoughts about which we need to exercise prayerful discrimination. Some of the thoughts that enter consciousness are nourishing and worthy of our attention, some are not. Those that are not—useless and dangerous willful, won'tful, fearful, wishful, shouldful thoughts—need to be sorted out and flushed away with floods of truth from Fundamental Mind. Prayer is flushing. Flush, and flush often. It doesn't take long, but it needs to be attended to regularly.

There is a time for this and a time for that—a time for contemplative prayer and a time for living prayer. Every moment and every circumstance has prayer potential. A man had trouble sleeping at night. He would drop off to sleep quickly, but then in an hour or so he would wake up and not be able to go back to sleep for worrying about how important it was for him to hurry and get back to sleep so that he would be in shape in the morning. To him I said, "So you mean everyone is sleeping, and there you are trying to run the world from your bed?" I recommended that he get up at such times, open a spiritually sound book, and be available to whatever would reveal itself.

Another who couldn't sleep reported that when she got up to pray at night she would begin by writing down her thoughts and then go through a long process of study and prayer for maybe two or three hours. Her prayer was mostly an attempt to exercise mental mastery over herself and her experience. There was no

God in it at all. To her I said, "Next time don't pray. Just get up and do something useful, like cleaning the toilet." Cleaning the toilet was a way of getting her off the throne and putting her to work in the service of God.

To serve and obey any intelligent idea rather than a worried, fretful one is really, for a moment, to trust God. This is why when I am least peaceful, I find that the most helpful prayer for me is, "What use does God have for me at this moment?" It is a way of letting go of the worrying by letting go into Fundamental Mind.

I have learned that nighttime awakenings can be very important. If I find myself awake in the middle of the night, I am almost glad if I don't fall right back to sleep. I am glad because I know something valuable is about to come to my attention. Whether needless worry awakens me or I just mysteriously find myself awake, if I don't drift back to sleep within a few minutes, I always get out of bed full of expectation. I put on my robe, wash my face, brush my teeth, go downstairs, and sit in a chair. Sometimes I open a book for inspiration, sometimes I just sit quietly and wait. I wait to see what comes to mind that I might need to consider—and something meaningful nearly always does. If not, if I am too full of thought-taking to hear the still small voice, then I get up and turn to living prayer, asking what use God has for me at this moment and then carrying out the message that comes—be it to start a certain business letter, fold a little laundry, or go back to bed. I am never tired in the morning after such a wakeful night.

The Value of Verbal Prayer

Many people pray by "talking to God" in the hope of persuading God to do what they want done. But by now it should be clear that the purpose of prayer is to listen to God. So if we are trying to listen to God, the question is whether there is any validity to "saying prayers"? Jesus taught us a prayer—the Lord's Prayer. Certainly verbal prayer has a place in our spiritual awakening—not for telling God what to do, but to help us become still and attentive. Meditation on a verbal prayer can be a way of banging the gavel in consciousness, shutting up to listen.

Earlier we noticed that we are engaged in false prayer most of the time. The way we do this is by constantly mumbling to ourselves about what we want and how to get it. If we did it out loud, they'd lock us up. What is the subject of all this talk? Ourselves. Mine the kingdom and the power and the glory. Or as someone I knew once said, "In the beginning, Ed."

In true prayer we aim to stop talking long enough to hear what someone is saying. To hear what someone is saying, it is first necessary to be interested enough to pay attention. The Bible says, "Before they call, I answer." God is talking to us all the time, but we drown him out with our mumbling, thought-taking prayers. However, trying not to think about something is the surest way to keep it fixed in mind. So it is helpful to focus our supposed minds on truthful, valid ideas, or on a truthful formal prayer such as the Lord's Prayer. This helps to drown out our own mumbling and draw our attention in the right direction.

When, whether aloud or in silence, we say such a prayer, we are not really talking to God. We are really still talking to ourselves, but now in spiritually valid terms. It is helpful to go slowly through the prayer, carefully seeking to understand and to see its relevancy to our immediate life experience until, finally, some truthful idea captures our attention and we begin to lose ourselves in it. At that moment the mumbling ceases. We have momentarily changed the subject of our lives from "me" to God. It is a powerful, power-filled moment because whatever is uppermost in consciousness is what will prevail in our lives.

Thus fulfilling, even so briefly, the first commandment to love God above all, we become still. And into that stillness God pours himself as love and intelligence and peace and often the precisely needed idea for that specific moment. At the same instant we become ourselves the beneficial, intelligent words God is uttering into the world. And as we proceed with our daily affairs, we suddenly find we are inspired and enlivened, and that all things are working together for good.

IF above all in consciousness we behold
> Our Father (Fundamental Mind, Source and
> Substance of all being) who art in heaven

THEN do we see
> thy kingdom come
> thy will be done
> on earth (in fact and experience)
> as it is in heaven (in truth and reality)

And that thou
> give us this day (from moment to moment)
> our daily bread (spiritual nourishment and
> inspiration)
> and forgive us our trespassings (indebtings)
> as (then are) we (also able to)
> forgive our debtors (trespassers).

And that thou
> Lead (lettest) us not (fall) into temptation
> But deliverest us from evil

FOR (BECAUSE)
> *thine* is the kingdom
> and the power
> and the glory
> forever and ever.

Check for Messages

In addition to three regular prayer times a day, it is important to touch base with Fundamental Mind frequently. A large part of our task is simply to begin to discover that Fundamental Mind exists. We encounter the presence of Fundamental Mind every time we are aware of receiving an inspired or needed idea. We can have such an encounter any time we look for one. Books and writings can be very helpful, and there are a great many good ones. You can discover some of my favorites by checking the footnotes for the various quotations I have selected. And there are a great many others to be discovered serendipitously.

As a springboard for prayer and meditation, one book I particularly like is *The Runner's Bible,* a small collection of Bible verses interspersed with brief, inspired commentary. For many years I have kept copies in convenient places, for my own daily practice of staying in touch with God. In moments of transition, as when going out the door, or changing from one task to another, I open the book at random—almost as if checking my mailbox. I look briefly at what catches my attention, consider its meaning, and see if there is any way in which it is particularly applicable to that moment of my life. (There always is!) Then I proceed, conducting my life as much as possible in accordance with what I have understood.

The Runner's Bible was originally prepared by a parent for her increasingly "on the go" teenage daughter. My teenage sons also find that things go more smoothly when they take time to duck into this little book "to see if there is any message there for me." (There always is.) More and more I see that Fundamental Mind is omnipresent and omnipotent. So more and more moments of my life are lived in direct, prayerful reference to its still small voice, which does not depend on book or doctrine or deed for expression. But so far I have not outgrown the benefits of such a book.

14. Now See Here

I want to beg you, as much as I can, to be patient toward all that is unsolved in your heart and to try to love the *questions themselves* like locked rooms and like books that are written in a very foreign tongue. Do not now seek the answers which cannot be given you because you would not be able to live them. And the point is, to live everything. *Live* the questions now. Perhaps you will then gradually, without noticing it, live along some distant day into the answer.

Resolve to be always beginning—to be a beginner!

RAINER MARIA RILKE

The shapes of change
ai ai they take their time
asking what the dawn asks
giving the answers evening gives
till tomorrow moves in
saying to man the moon shooter
"now I am here—now read me—
give me a name."

CARL SANDBURG

We began with the plan to take a trip together. Now here we are at the end of it, and what we have seen on this whole trip is that the only trip is from dreaming to waking. Those roads out of town that we were going to travel—it really doesn't matter if we take them or not. For even if we do, they will bring us home again to the life before us and the task of waking up in it. So here is a ticket for that ultimate non-trip. It is, of course, a prayer.

Now that we have a better understanding of what true spiritual prayer is, this is an easy prayer to begin on: *Now see here.* It is one of the shortest prayers I know. It is my aspirin bottle and vitamin capsule and booster shot. It has two meanings. One is a slap in the face: *Wake up, sleepyhead. Stop this nonsense. Pay attention. Stop feeling sorry for yourself. Stop drifting. Get with it!* Sometimes that is all I need to hear—the silent no-nonsense of, *Now (for God's sake) see here!* But each word also has profound, truthful significance to be helpfully considered by tracing it back to God in contemplative prayer.

Now

Now. We do not *need* to look ahead. "Take no thought for the morrow." We need to *not* look ahead. If we look ahead too hard, we start to become heads again with minds inside trying to have an overview, reaching in all directions, getting all tangled and caught up and strung out. The tendency is to rush ahead after a *what if. What if* I can't? *What if* they won't? These "what ifs" lure and threaten us into the future, making us take thought for ourselves and drowning out the thoughts that God is having for us. But we aren't there yet. All the time that we are trying to make a better future by being against the past, we are missing each real moment of life at hand. Wait until the time comes. Now just see here. Isn't there enough to go on for now?

We also do not need to look back and stay depressed over loss, bitter over disappointments, guilty and ashamed over former words and deeds. If the past was good, it was good at the time. The new good of now is even better for now. If we remember the past only as bad, we can be sure that we did not recognize the good of what was then the present. To rectify past bitterness toward others and guilt toward self, start seeing the good of now. Otherwise this now, too, will become a regrettable waste.

One woman reached a difficult time in her life when her children were grown and out of the house. She and her husband decided to remodel their kitchen. When that was finished, she expected to "relax a little and enjoy life." But just then her husband's business failed, and he decided to retire. The wife didn't know what to do. She found it difficult to have her husband home all day, and they needed money. Sometimes she felt resentful and afraid. She didn't want to go to work and didn't know what she could do anyway, since her original skills were not up to date. The kitchen renovation was not going well; and with her husband depressed, the task of dealing with the workers fell largely on her shoulders. It seemed so pointless. Why remodel the kitchen when they needed money? Soon after the remodeling was done it became apparent that maintaining the house was too difficult. They decided to move to a condominium in another town. This, too, seemed pointless and discouraging. Just when their children were gone and their house remodeled, why move away from their friends to a strange place?

But through all these questions and changes and ups and downs she kept praying and letting go and trusting in Fundamental Mind, living moment by moment according to the best that she could see. The sale of the house was effortless and, because of the new kitchen, far more profitable than they had dreamed. Within a week she was offered a part-time job in the office of their new condominium. Though she took the job just to help out financially and to get out of the house, she discovered that she loved the work and was able to learn word processing, a task she found fascinating. Her new work entailed many skills she had just acquired through the process of remodeling the kitchen. After many years of working out of the house, the husband found new enjoyment at home. They found themselves enjoying a whole new life together. "To think," she said, "that a few months ago I couldn't see the point of anything. But everything that looked like loss turned out to be gain. Everything that looked like the end turned out to be a beginning. Everything that looked bad turned out to be good!"

It is not what happens good or ill that is so important. It is not even doing well that matters. What is important is what we see and whether we see God. For in all our experiences good or ill, it is the presence of God that is being brought to our attention. In her ninetieth year Frances Wickes wrote:

I have lived . . . long enough to see that life and death are not interested in the finished product that has "turned out" this way or that way; but are concerned with the eternal process of being and becoming . . . a process where the unexpected is forever breaking through the pattern of the seemingly established, and at every turn of the river of life new vistas may be opened, enabling the soul to glimpse that country where ultimate mysteries, unknown and unknowable, abide. . . . We know that we do not know. Yet with the passing of long, long years, if we have really lived and not just gone through the accepted motions of living, we have learned to distinguish, with clearer vision, between those experiences which are transitory and those that are eternal and lead into greater understanding of the timeless realities of the soul.[1]

If you go to the theater for the first time and have balcony seats, you may be startled by how steep the balcony is, how dark it is between you and your seat. You feel as if you might stumble and fall right off the balcony into the audience below. But every few feet there is a light close to the floor. From the top of the stairs you cannot see your seat, but you can see the next few steps. When you have gone a few steps, there is a new light for the next few. So instead of trying to see all the way to where you are going, you look at the next step. The next step is always clear. The mind of God provides us with everything needed for each next moment.

Now is the time. There is no place or time in the water where buoyancy will not support us, no circumstance in life in which God will not uphold us. But the only time and place when the water will hold us up is now and here. And the only time and place when God upholds us is now and here. Now. See. Here. Stop holding on. Behold, and be upheld.

See

See. Now *see* here. We can be guided by the light at our feet only if we are paying attention to just the next step, looking within the light, seeing by it. When we pray along the lines of *now see here*, we are not seeking to get or hang onto or control things, but to recognize what is—right here and now.

When I was a child, I discovered the fun of running down mountains. I was warned that this was dangerous. But I had discovered a secret. Even on a rugged trail it was possible to run safely if you simply focused on each next step and did not look farther ahead. There was always a landing place for one foot. At any moment I needed to see only one landing place for one foot. One step at a time. As a growing-up child of God, I am discovering that there is always enough guidance for the living of this moment. I am learning not to try to look beyond the light.

Only two things are ever happening: the truth proving itself true, the false proving itself false. If I have a problem, the problem signifies either a mistaken belief or a lack of understanding. Sometimes there is "something that can be done about it," sometimes not. But whether there is or isn't, "doing something" is never enough. There is always something that needs to be learned, to be *seen*. Sometimes this better seeing erases even the appearance of a problem, but whether it does or doesn't, we are always better off and in a higher place when we have come to a clearer understanding of truth. So the answer is never simply to do something about the problem, but to see better, replacing error or ignorance with truth.

But suppose things are not going well. How can we approach this gratefully? Only from the standpoint of seeing? Suppose you are working on an electronic calculator or computer. You push a lot of buttons to put in information and instructions, and wait for the machine to do the work. The display on the screen lights up and you see that the answer is wrong, or a message lights up that says ERROR. You may be disappointed, but you do not get angry at the display. You do not send the computer back to the factory because it doesn't work. Instead you list your program. You retrace and reexamine your entries. You are looking for an error or a higher understanding. You say, "What could manifest itself in a display like that?" or "What can be learned here?"

As unmercifully painful as they sometimes are, life's lessons and error messages are the essence of divine mercy. We can't help wishing to be excused from the side effects of our errors and ignorance. We would love to be protected from the lessons, that is, to have God make an exception in our case. But if that were possible, God wouldn't be God, Fundamental Mind wouldn't be Fundamental Mind, and there would be no mercy and no hope for anyone—and nothing at all to count on. Without problems, we would never get to the truth, never find fulfillment and love. How much easier and richer our lives are, how much easier we are on each other, when we see our experiences as displays of error or ignorance and as opportunities for spiritual growth! When we find ourselves in conflict, instead of justifying, retaliating, blaming, or changing each other, we can say, "Is *this* love? No, this *can't* be love. Hmm, what idea could manifest itself in an experience like this?" When we are grieving or hurt, we can pray, "What do I need to see?" So we look for new insight and inspiration. And that is when it comes. That is, after all, how we learned to walk on earth. I suppose it is how to walk in heaven as well. God always wants to show us more. And whenever we see it, life is always better. "Eye hath not seen nor ear heard the things that God hath planned for those that love him."[2]

Jesus said, "The eye is the lamp of the body; if then the light that is in you is darkness, how great is that darkness . . . But if thine eye be *single* thy whole body [thy whole *being*, thy whole *life!*] shall be full of light."[3] When we trace everything back to God, we are seeing with a single eye. How we see is the determining factor in our lives. It determines how we are, and to some extent even how life happens to us. So it is much better to be concerned with seeing what is than with getting or doing or feeling something that should-be-but-isn't. What do I need to see now? This is truly enough. We are not knowers/tellers but see-ers/be-ers, expressions of what we are aware of. This is what we are. So when we look to see, we are claiming our true lives. This is the life. Seeing is being.

Song of the Seeing Being

The more we see that seeing is the issue in life,
the more we look at everything for what it has to teach us.
The more we look at everything for what it has to teach us,
the more we see that we are being taught.
The more we see that we are being taught,
the more we know that we are loved.
The more we know that we are loved,
the more lovingly we are seeing.
The more lovingly we are seeing,
the more loving we are being.

The more loving we are being,
the more we see that seeing is the issue in life.
    . . . (*start over*)[4]

A wonderful early benefit to looking at life in this way is the advent of meaning to one's life. There come times when each of us asks, "Does my life have any meaning?" Usually this occurs when we are experiencing sadness, failure, pain, or anxiety. There may be tremendous darkness, overwhelming despair. The thought comes that it isn't worth it, that it would be nice to just quit. Until we look at everything for what it has to teach us, it is as if we were just reacting to the display on the computer. When we like what lights up, we get happy. When we don't like it, we get angry or depressed. Or we try to change the display in a certain way—and then we get frustrated.

But when we look for meaning, suddenly life is meaningful. Jesus looked at life as meaningful, as significant. To him everything was either a display of truth (in which case it was good) or a display of illusion or error (in which case he sought to understand and get beyond the illusion), or an opportunity in which he could look forward to realizing something important. He looked at a man who had been paralyzed his whole life, but he just didn't buy it. He perceived that the man was paralyzed by his thought. Even on the cross he was looking through evil to see God's good. So he prays one moment, "Why hast thou forsaken me?" which I take to mean, "Why did you let them do this to me?" And in the next moment he says, "Forgive them, Lord, for they know not what they do," which I take to mean that he saw that what they did to him was ultimately nothing personal. So when Jesus looked at bad things, instead of thinking how terrible they were, he would be asking their significance and seeking new understanding. He valued understanding even more than he wanted to avoid unpleasant experience.

A great thing about this significance-seeing approach to everyday life is that it helps us benefit from both "good" and "bad" experiences. If we approach a bad experience this way, we discover the error or ignorance behind it, which is the first step in getting free of it, of separating the thinker from the thought. On the other hand, if we approach something good and harmonious in this way, we find Fundamental Mind in the background. This way our consciousness of God's presence keeps expanding and we grow increasingly grateful, assured, and free. Now everything that happens is either a blessing that is also a lesson, or a lesson that is also a blessing. I call them both "blessons."

Fulfillment and happiness do not depend on whether an experience pleases us, nor on any reaction we make to the experience itself. Everything depends on our understanding of the significance of things, which in turn is the key to bringing ourselves into conscious alignment with the invisible laws of being, which in turn will be manifest as otherwise inexpressible love, beauty, and meticulous perfection.

Whenever life seems meaningless, we are not in fact looking for meaning. We are just reacting to our experience (the display) and thinking of what we want, what we suppose we know is best. Meaning disappears when wanting takes over. But then the problem isn't really meaninglessness; it's the temper tantrum, the blind rage that won't see good. That this is selfish and egotistical is almost beside the point. The point is that it is completely missing the point—and the pointing! Through our computer analogy we see how pointless this orientation is, because no understanding is taking place, and life remains chancy, pointless, and meaningless. We are just victims of whatever shows up on the screen.

But when we look to see, suddenly meaning is everywhere. Now, besides increased understanding, we encounter the immediate benefit that the little (and big) spells of meaninglessness that once plagued us mysteriously become rare. This is really a tremendous blessing. Enlightenment is a lifelong process. You don't just get enlightened and then live that way. All through life there will be lessons. Eventually we can learn to trust and love the endless unfolding of meaning.

Here

Here. Like the duck in the poem, we must "ease ourselves into the boundless just where it touches us." *This* is my life. If I miss God in the here and now, I have missed a moment of my life. Thrown it away. Slowly, surely, simply, purely. Every moment is an opportunity for existential prayer. Right here is where either life or illusion is taking place. If illusion is present, we are most likely in difficulty. But even this difficulty is the best place to be, because it is our gate to the kingdom, a private entrance. *This* is where illusion is proving itself false, so this is the place where we can wake from it to God. Now see *here.* "This is the day that the Lord hath made; let us rejoice and be glad in it."[5] "Behold, now is the acceptable time; behold, now is the day of salvation."[6] This is *the* moment that the Lord hath made. Wherever we are, no matter what is before us, good or bad, "The place whereon thou standest is holy ground."[7] Awareness is the key. Either we wake up now, or we go on dreaming—and suffering. This is when and where, through our reliance, God ceases to be a wish or a theory and becomes a reliable force in our lives. Most of all, this is when and where we can become its evidence in the world. The eye is the lamp of the individual. We are the light of the world. Whatever we put in charge of consciousness one moment gains momentum in the next. One moment of awareness leads to another.

Many believe it is helpful to "get away from it all" in order to "become enlightened." But if God is God, this is not only true in monasteries and Himalayan caves, but also in everyday life. Although we need at times to distance ourselves from others, Jesus never withdrew from society for long. He knew that this "here" is it.

Zen Buddhist masters give their students bewildering riddles called *koans* to solve. They are not solved, really, but seen through, *dis*solved, as the student awakens to higher levels of awareness. In the Judeo-Christian tradition all life is a riddle to be seen through. There is no place to go for more individualized training than right here in our own life as it is popping up around us. From the moment we wake up each morning every circumstance is our opportunity to see and to express the fact and force and nature of Fundamental Mind as loving mentor. There is no better place to be than here. Here is where we are closest to God and God is closest to us.

Pearl S. Buck tells of a ship becalmed at sea for such a long time that the supply of drinking water ran out and people began to die of thirst. Days later a freighter appeared on the horizon. The survivors did everything possible to attract attention. At last the freighter drew close. "Please, give us some water," begged the captain. "We are dying of thirst." But the other captain called out, "Put down your buckets where you are!" Days before, the ship had drifted into fresh water. All the time that they had been struggling to get water and dying of thirst, they had been sitting in fresh water!

As Good as It Gets

> One moment is as God as another
> One place is as God as another.
> One task is as God as another.
> One life is as God as another

A Zen master was asked what it was like to be enlightened. He said, "I eat when I'm hungry. I sleep when I'm tired."

"But isn't that what everyone does?" the questioner asked.

"Oh, no!" said the master. "When others eat, they think of ten thousand things. When they sleep, they dream of ten thousand things. When I eat, I just eat. When I sleep, I just sleep."

A young mother described to me a moment of this "Now See Here" consciousness.

We were sitting in Brooklyn on the front stoop, my husband, our two-year-old daughter, and I. My daughter was in her party dress. Amazingly, even though she had worn it to a party, it was still clean. So we thought, maybe if we put her in a raincoat to eat this ice cream cone, she can keep her dress clean for one more wearing. There she was in her raincoat in the hot sun, and the ice cream was running all over the place. She was a complete mess. And it didn't matter. It was so wonderful. "You know, Mark," I said to my husband, "I think this is as good as it gets."

You may say, so what? Big deal! Why shouldn't she enjoy watching her daughter eat ice cream? She had no big problems to worry about. But that's exactly what I like about this story. Because, in fact, we almost always think we have something more important to worry about, so we are almost never aware of the fact that at least for this one moment everything is perfect.

That's what this story is all about. She had no mental tentacles out, no thought strings of false connecting prayer. She could have been thinking ten thousand thoughts: *When will my daughter learn not to be a slob? This is embarrassing! What will the neighbors think of her wearing such a warm coat in August? Watch out! It's dripping! Watch out! All the ice cream is going to waste! What am I doing wasting my time here when I have so much more important work to do before I go to the office tomorrow? Before she was born we had more sex. More better sex. We could be having sex right now, right in the middle of the afternoon. It used to be so nice. Maybe it was a mistake to have a baby. Why didn't my husband let me change her clothes before giving her ice cream? He's not the one that does the laundry. Why should I always have to be the one to do the laundry? He should do it. My daughter is getting too hot in that raincoat. She shouldn't have so much sugar. Maybe she'll grow up to be spoiled. Surely she will have rotten teeth. What if she gets acne? What if she has diabetes? She should have better manners by now. Maybe she's retarded! I have other more important things to do than to be sitting around here. What are we going to have for supper? Which of us is going to fix it? Who's going to go to the store?*

But *none* of these thoughts were in her mind. No mental tentacles. No false connecting prayers. She was just there, overjoyed by the goodness of being with her beautiful husband and her beautiful daughter with beautiful ice cream running down beautifully all over the beautiful place. Now! See! Here! For the child of God at any age, this is as good as it gets. This is always as good as it gets. Compared to "octopus consciousness," we could call this "lotus consciousness"—just one long root dangling down into the deep, and the flower floating and quietly opening on the surface.

No matter how terrible our predicament or how pressing our concerns, in spiritual prayer we momentarily set aside all impressions of what we seem to be and where we seem to be and what seems to be going on and what we think we want and need and what we think we are for—in order to allow ourselves to be inspired with a realization of our true spiritual nature, context, and purpose in life. Now. See. Here. Trace *this* now back to God. Is God nowhere to be found? Is there no trace of God to be found in our lives? No sign of God that we can recognize and manifest? Then it is we who are missing. We are absent-minded, out of our true Mind.

God is *nowhere* to be found? God is *now here* to be found! Now see here. See here now. Here now, see. The gate is narrow that leads to the kingdom. It is the O in the middle of Now. When we have pulled in all our mental tentacles, we become quite small. We become a hole in the middle of Now, a hole where God shines through. We are so small, so nothing, that we can slip right through the O of Now, the narrow gate into heaven. Right where we were a moment ago, now God is shining into the world. So, occasionally we wake up for a moment. Now, and again, now. We are the light of the world. Indeed, it was not with our fathers that the Lord made this covenant, but with us who are all of us here alive this day. This is indeed the day that the Lord hath made; let us be glad and rejoice in it!

We have to start sometime. Now! We have to start somehow. See! We have to start somewhere. Here!

Notes

1. Finding the Road That Leads to the Road

Epigraph. D. T. Suzuki, *Manual of Zen Buddhism* (New York: Grove Press, 1960), 82.

Epigraph. Meister Eckhart, in Raymond Bernard Blakney, *Meister Eckhart, A Modern Translation* (New York: Harper & Row, 1941), 75.

1. Deuteronomy 6:4. With one noted exception, all biblical quotes in this work have been taken from either the King James or the Revised Standard Version of the Bible. In a few instances I have paraphrased to avoid unnecessary sexism, but only where I felt there was no resulting distortion or awkwardness.
2. Deuteronomy 5:3.
3. Seng T'san, in Edward Conze, ed., *Buddhist Scriptures* (Harmondsworth, Middlesex, England: Penguin, 1919), 174.
4. John 10:30.

2. Dying to Wake Up

Epigraph. Maya Angelou, *I Know Why the Caged Bird Sings* (New York: Random House, 1969), 264.

1. Truman Capote, *A Christmas Memory* (New York: Random House, 1956), 42–43.
2. 1 Kings 19:12.
3. Psalms 139:7–8.
4. Proverbs 23:7.
5. P. Lal, trans., *The Dhammapada* (New York: Farrar, Straus & Giroux, 1967), 39.
6. Hosea 11:1–4.

3. Is There Life Beyond Coping?

Epigraph. Lao Tzu, in Stephen Mitchell, *The Tao Te Ching, A New Version* (New York: Harper & Row, 1988), 74.

1. Erma Bombeck, *Motherhood: The Second Oldest Profession* (New York: McGraw Hill, 1981), 44–45.
2. Romans 7:19.
3. Joseph Campbell, with Bill Moyers, *The Power of Myth* (New York: Doubleday, 1988), 107.

4. Yearning to Make Connections

Epigraph. Igjugarjuk, in Joseph Campbell, *The Masks of God: Primitive Mythology* (New York: The Viking Press, 1959), 5, from H. Ostermann, *The Alaskan Eskimos, as described in the posthumous Notes of Dr. Knud Rasmussen, Report of the Fifth Thule Expedition 1921–24,* vol. X, No. 3 (Copenhagen: Nordisk Forlag, 1952), 97.

Epigraph. Robert Frost, *In the Clearing* (New York: Holt, Rinehart & Winston, 1962), 39.

1. See D. W. Winnicot, *The Maturational Processes and the Facilitating Environment,* (New York: International Universities Press, 1965). The parental inclination to reassure their infants that they are not on their own by being lovingly present is good and necessary. However, this parental presence can become overbearing and deprive a child of early peaceful solitude. As Winnicot points out, children who are allowed to be alone in someone's loving, non-interfering presence also develop the capacity to be alone by themselves.

2. Sometimes when people feel hurt or let down by others, or when they believe others stand in the way of their happiness, they conclude that happiness depends on their getting away from others. So they go off by themselves and "have no use" for people. However, this, too, is a form of people dependency. There is still a background thought that one should and would like to be able to count on others but cannot. If either the presence or the absence of others is regarded as a condition of one's well-being there is still other-dependency.

3. *New York Times* (August 17, 1981), 2:12:2.

4. This personal idea of God is more limited than Fundamental Mind. It is a swayable, temperamental, unreliable, human-like concept of God. It is an idea of God that is modeled after our parents. Expanding the idea of God to more than a person does not obviate the possibility of knowing oneself to be loved and cared for by God. On the contrary it makes awareness of true, reliable divine love possible. See chapter 10 for further discussion of God's love.

5. John 4:13.

5. Seeing Through Life's Betrayals

Epigraph. Stephen Mitchell, ed. and trans., *The Selected Poetry of Rainer Maria Rilke* (New York: Random House, 1980), 245.

1. In this book I have not attempted to deal with the presence of Eve in the creation story, neither because she is unimportant nor out of any sexist bias. We are not concerned here with gender but with the origin of consciousness and self-consciousness. The exclusive focus on Adam here is not as a gender model but as the representative of the human species, male and female. Consideration of Adam and Eve as male and female belongs more properly to a work devoted to human nature and love. Such a discussion would examine the male and female "sides" of every individual and explore love as the mutual fulfillment of these potentials by both men and women.

6. The Illusion of Growing Up

Epigraph. Gerald May, *Will and Spirit* (San Francisco: Harper & Row, 1987), 1–2.

1. In Hebrew it was actually a "fruit" that Adam picked. Not until the Latin Vulgate edition of the Christian Bible did the fruit become an apple. According to W. Gunther Plaut in *Commentaries on Genesis, Exodus, Leviticus, Numbers, and Deuteronomy* (New York: The Union of American Hebrew

Congregations, 1981), this choice was made because the apple was popular in Europe, and because the Latin translation of evil is *malum*, which also means *apple*, while *malus* means both *bad* and *apple tree*. Horticulturists suggest that the fruit was probably an apricot, while Jewish tradition suggests grape, fig, or citron.

2. Genesis 3:5.
3. Matthew 6:25.
4. 2 Corinthians 2:9.
5. Ecclesiastes 7:29.
6. John 3:19.

7. Discovering a Spiritual Viewpoint

Epigraph. Wendell Berry, *Collected Poems 1957–1982* (San Francisco: North Point Press, 1985), 145.
Epigraph. From the *Mundaka*, in Hugh l'Anson Fausset, *The Flame and the Light* (Wheaton, IL: The Theosophical Publishing House, 1958), 56.

1. Some readers may object to the fact that I have not attempted to work around the seeming sexism of calling God the Father, rather than, say, Father/Mother, or Parent. The masculine designation of the deity in the early religion of the Hebrew people may have been in reaction to disorderly, sensual extremes of more feminine religions. While limitations of describing God only in masculine terms certainly need to be transcended, the original choice of a masculine God may well have been an attempt to establish order by discovering roots in truth and principle. It is only through putting down such conscious roots that the harmony recognizable as divine love can be realized. In any case it was only natural for Jesus as a Jew to think of God in masculine terms. In recognizing God as his parent and realizing his oneness with it, Jesus (born of a divine father, but still a human mother) stands at the very point at which intelligence (a traditionally masculine principle) becomes recognizable as reliable love (a traditionally feminine principle). Now John can be the first to say that God is love. Now we can begin to know that God is both father and mother.
2. Joseph Campbell said that when he first started to teach mythology to college students he was worried that he would shake their faith in the religious tradition in which they had been raised. He found instead that awareness of other traditions only served to deepen their faith.
3. Romans 12:2.
4. D. T. Suzuki, *Introduction to Zen Buddhism* (New York: Harper & Row, 1949).
5. Albert Einstein, *Autobiographical Note*, translated and edited by Paul Arthur Schilpp (Chicago: Open Court Publishing, 1979), 9.
6. John 7:24.
7. 2 Corinthians 4:18.
8. Stanley Goldberg, "Albert Einstein and the Creative Act: The Case of Special Relativity," in Aris Rutherford, H. Ted Davis, and Roger H. Streuer, eds., *Springs of Scientific Creativity* (Minneapolis: University of Minnesota Press, 1983), 232.
9. Heinz Pagels, *Perfect Symmetry* (New York: Simon & Schuster, 1985), 362.
10. Matthew 5:17.

11. Matthew 19:17.
12. John 5:19.
13. John 5:17.
14. John 14:9.
15. Jeremiah 31:34.
16. John 14:12.
17. John 4:32, 34.
18. John 2:5.
19. Matthew 19:17.
20. John 5:17.
21. John 5:17.
22. Luke 17:21.
23. John 7:24.
24. John 8:32.

8. Guided by Living Compasses

Epigraph. Issa, translated by Robert Hass, in Stephen Mitchell, *The Enlightened Heart* (New York: Harper & Row, 1989), 99.
1. Polly Berrien Berends, *Whole Child/Whole Parent* (New York: Harper & Row, 1974; rev. ed. 1983), 290.
2. Source unknown.
3. Matthew 6:22.
4. John 5:19.
5. Albert Einstein, in Abraham Pais, *"Subtle Is the Lord . . . "* (New York: Oxford University Press, 1982), 57.
6. *Ibid.*, 443.
7. *Ibid.*, 30.
8. *Ibid.*, front matter.
9. Matthew 22:37; Mark 12:29–30.
10. Matthew 6:22.
11. John 16:12.
12. Matthew 8:20.
13. Luke 2:49.
14. Matthew 4:10; Luke 4:8.
15. P. Lal, trans., *The Dhammapada* (New York: Farrar, Straus & Giroux, 1967), 13.
16. Joseph Campbell, with Bill Moyers, *The Power of Myth* (New York: Doubleday, 1988), 118.
17. "Lay not up for yourselves treasure upon earth, where moth and rust corrupt, and where thieves break in and steal" (Matthew 6:19); "they . . . love the uppermost rooms at feasts, and the chief seats in the synagogues, and greetings in the markets, and to be called Rabbi, Rabbi. But be ye not called Rabbi, for one is your master . . . " (Matthew 23:7); "And he sent forth his servants to call them that were bidden to the wedding: and they would not come. But they made light of it and went their ways, one to his farm, another to his merchandise . . . " (Matthew 22:3,5).
18. Buddha, in Lal, *The Dhammapada*, 157.
19. Mark 4:19.
20. Matthew 6:24.

21. Matthew 12:30; Luke 11:23.
22. Matthew 22:38.
23. Albert Einstein, quoted in Pais, *"Subtle Is the Lord,"* 27.
24. Matthew 7:29; Mark 1:22.
25. Willa Cather, *My Antonia* (Boston: Houghton Mifflin, 1918), 7–8.
26. *Ibid.*, 14.

9. Universal Firsthand Realizations of Oneness

Epigraph. Thomas Traherne, in Anne Ridler, *Thomas Traherne, Poems, Centuries and Three Thanksgivings* (London: Oxford University Press, 1966), 16.
Epigraph. Rainer Maria Rilke, in Stephen Mitchell, ed. and trans., *The Selected Poetry of Rainer Maria Rilke* (New York: Random House, 1980), 259.
1. John 5:19.
2. Matthew 14:28.
3. When I was a student at Union Theological Seminary there were still students there who had taken courses with Dr. Tillich. One of the stories they liked to tell was about how confused everyone was when in a lecture he kept repeating, "There is no face without noses." It was, of course, his heavy German accent that caused the confusion. What he said was, "Zere is no fayz vizout gnosis." *Gnosis* is Greek for *understanding*. What he meant was, "There is no faith without understanding."
4. Matthew 10:39.
5. Matthew 6:26, 30–31.
6. John 7:24.
7. John 1:14.
8. Matthew 14:29–31.
9. Luke 23:46.
10. Ruth Berrien Fox, *A Catch or Key* (Peterborough, NH: Noone House, William L. Bauhan, Publisher, 1969), 40.
11. Romans 8:28.
12. Polly Berrien Berends, *Whole Child/Whole Parent* (New York: Harper & Row, 1974; rev. ed. 1983), 9.
13. Mark 10:15.
14. D. T. Suzuki, in Eugen Herrigel, *Zen and the Art of Archery* (New York: Random House, 1953), 11.
15. John 3:3–5.
16. 1 Corinthians 15:22.

10. The Need to Be Reminded

Epigraph. Donald C. Babcock, from "The Little Duck," *The New Yorker* (October 4, 1947): 39.
1. Acts 17:27–28.
2. Huston Smith, *The Religions of Man* (New York: Harper & Row, 1958), 90.
3. Wendell Berry, *Remembering* (San Francisco: North Point Press, 1988) 32–33.
4. *Ibid.*, 58–59.
5. 1 John 4:8.
6. Psalms 139:7–10.

7. Romans 8:38–39.
8. 1 Corinthians 12:21.
9. Acts 17:28.
10. 1 Corinthians 2:9.
11. 1 Thessalonians 5:17.

11. False Prayer: Avoiding the Void

Epigraph. Rudyard Kipling, "The Seal Lullabye," from *The Jungle Book* (New York: Macmillan & Co., 1948).
1. This story has been freely adapted from an anecdote in Bhagwan Shree Rajneesh, *The Mustard Seed* (New York: Harper & Row, 1975), 315.
2. Psalms 46:10; Proverbs 3:6.
3. With slight variations, these lyrics by Anna L. Waring appear in a number of different hymnals, including The Hymnal of the Protestant Episcopal Church 1940, The Pilgrim Hymnal, and The Christian Science Hymnal.
4. Pamela Gray, in Mary Strong, ed., *Letters of the Scattered Brotherhood* (New York: Harper & Row, 1948), 8.
5. James 4:3.

12. At Prayer and Aware: Dynamics of True Prayer

1. Psalms 121:4.
2. Joshua 24:15.
3. Thomas Hora, *Existential Metapsychiatry* (New York: Seabury Press, 1977), 91.
4. 1 Samuel 3:9.
5. Psalms 100:3.
6. Isaiah 30:21.
7. Isaiah 65:24.
8. James 1:22.
9. I am told that studies suggest that most of these survivors had good homes before the disaster, whereas those who were not so well situated do not make it through the horrors nearly so well, if at all. Those who had wise, caring parents in early childhood recognize wise, loving guidance coming from out of the blue.
10. Psalms 131.
11. Luke 6:37.
12. John 16:33.

13. The Practice of Prayer

Epigraph. Hugh l'Anson Fausset, *The Flame and the Light* (Wheaton, IL: The Theosophical Publishing Society, 1958), 178–79.
1. John 1:13; 3:3, 5.
2. Matthew 6:5–6.

14. Now See Here

Epigraph. Rainer Maria Rilke, in John J. L. Mood, compiler, *Rilke on Love and Other Difficulties* (New York: W. W. Norton, 1975), 25.

Epigraph. Carl Sandburg, from "Man the Moon Shooter," in *Harvest Poems* (New York: Harcourt, Brace, Jovanovich, 1958), 125.

1. Frances Wickes, *The Inner World of Childhood* (Boston: Sigo Press, 1988), xiv.
2. Isaiah 64:4.
3. Matthew 6:22–23.
4. Polly Berrien Berends, *Whole Child/Whole Parent* (New York: Harper & Row, 1974; rev. ed. 1983), 56.
5. Psalms 118:24.
6. 2 Corinthians 6:2.
7. Exodus 3:5.